The Honorable Relationship

Publisher: LeeCore Corporation

Cover Design: Laura Imkamp

Wisdom is better than weapons of war...

Ecclesiastes 9:18 (KJV)

This book was a long time in the making and is dedicated to the following:

My mother, Mary, who gave me the spark of integrity and kept it aflame throughout my life

My father, Colby, who gave me the guidance and fortitude needed to navigate this world

My beautiful wife, Sandy, who loves me and sees the best in me and expects nothing less

Most of all, my Heavenly Father who has blessed me beyond measure and His Son Jesus who died for me!

Further Acknowledgement: I would like to thank Laura Imkamp, Dan O'Boyle, Sharon Schenk and Andrea Staargaard for their invaluable contributions to the making of this book.

Table of Contents

The Honorable Relationship

Preface

The Honorable Relationship originally came to life for two purposes. The first purpose is to show a better model wherein business relationships are created and fostered that will not only increase business revenue and opportunities but also promote longevity even in the worst of life's storms. The second purpose is to offer a template that promotes ethical relationships which are also effective relationships.

This project began many years prior to the tempest-tossed environment that we currently are experiencing and yet its arrival could not come at a better time. The dual forces of unprecedented economic havoc along with the terrible, seemingly conscience-less actions of leaders in business have left all of us with our mouths agape. The genesis of The Honorable Relationship was to improve revenue production (sales) approach but, in talking over with serious business professionals over the past years, it has become evident that the "knob has been broken off" in terms of the way business has been conducted.

Business has never been easy....never. However, there has emerged an astonishing de-personalization of people and companies that has created this extreme volatility and lack of: cohesiveness, fair-play, morality, and even civility. A scenario so bad that any of us can be told by a superior or client that even though we have been loyal throughout the years and worked hard and done very well for them, due to a better priced company that was sourced by a soulless procurement department, now we must part ways. And we are supposed to reasonably accept all this by the ending statement: "It isn't personal, it's just business".

WOW! Really? Is it just business? Or does that statement ring hollow much like the beleaguered boyfriend/girlfriend who when pressed by their counterpart as to why they want to break up, says with near exasperation, "It's not you, it's me!" Really? We all know better.

So, what can be done to correct the current state of affairs? What is clear is that there is a need for a better model of how to conduct oneself and one's company in the business world. In searching for a better model, what can we focus on? Since we have no capacity to look into the future, let's look to the past and see what DOES work and what IS right.

Let's look at a model that has not gone out of style (maybe just temporarily forgotten) but that is/was the bedrock of doing business from time immemorial. How did our parents, grandparents or ancestors conduct business and was it a good model?

Getting past the rose-colored lenses of nostalgia, I think it is fair to say that business in the past was conducted:

- Without lengthy contracts that had escape clauses riddled throughout the documents

- Without RFPs (Request for Proposals) selection committees and KPIs (Key Performance Indicators) and SLAs (Service Level Agreements) and all that nonsense

- Without accountants, attorneys, and, most of all, procurement officers making business decisions on behalf (or in place of) true business owners or operators

- With integrity and certain a leeway for forgiveness

Business wasn't done coldly and dispassionately, but rather it was PERSONAL and it was balanced.

Looking at it this way shows how far we have strayed from the paths our forefathers had walked -- the paths of competition and effectiveness, yes, but also those of honor and ethics. A model that would've worked well with two people sealing the "deal" by a handshake or by a contract written on the back of a cocktail napkin. Contracts that would stand for decades without any written codification? Is it a pipe dream?

How can we regain a semblance of this former reality once again? A return to a balanced way of doing business in the 21st century. It will require a quantum shift in thinking, viewing, and acting out how we conduct ourselves and our business.

It will require that we change EVERYTHING.

Section One:
The Honorable Relationship Philosophy

In looking at all the information being disseminated by experts in the business world, it seemed like a daunting task to write "one more business" book, especially in light of the fact that the authors all seemed to have such formidable backgrounds. However, in the process of working and interacting with clients, students, and my peers in the fields of consulting and sales, I realized that there exists a chasm between what is being taught by these experts and what is being applied every day by businesspeople of every stripe in the assortment of markets that exists today.

A lot of the business teachings promulgated nowadays range from techniques/methods-driven thinking to theoretical/ethical arguments and constructs. But they don't address fundamental issues that drive (or block) business effectiveness in real-world, applicable terms. Instead, the current teachings are either too process-driven or too theoretical. And if they do drive through the point of results then what are the results that are really being aimed at? The solutions proffered tend to be mechanical and amoral.

Isn't that what has brought us to where we currently are? "Do unto others then run" as the joke goes. But the financial and moral debacle that we are now seeing really takes the humor out of that quip. We need to stop thinking of business as a series of transactions that are disjointed efforts to fulfill "numbers" or "quotas" and that are based on the highest rate of return without ANY consequences to anyone. That kind of thinking is what brought us to where we now are – at the precipice of history.

Instead of a lot of recriminations and hand-wringing, what is needed is a collective personal resolve to change once and for all the kind of thinking that has permeated the business world up to now. We need a new way of looking at how to conduct business as it pertains to client management or business-to-business relations.

A new platform must be envisioned that will increase revenue, create balanced business relationships and keep ethics at a higher level. A platform of beneficial reciprocity and mutual load sharing instead of one-sided relationships or hit-

and-run approaches to doing business. The Honorable Relationship is a way of thinking and doing that is meant to do exactly that.

The Honorable Relationship is based on the most powerful engine of business that exists: relationships. Relationships are the real drivers in business. This has been true from antiquity to now and will continue to be so even when this generation passes on. The power of relationships cannot be overestimated. They may be in the form of partnerships (law firms), client relations (account management) and/or business-to-business types.

Without relationships there would be no trust and no collaborations, no matter how big or small. Relationships transcend market volatility and fads of the day and really good relationships are based on ethical constructs that help guide both parties so that no one goes astray.

The aim of this book is for you to be able to build up old relationships and help to create new relationships that will: increase revenue and market share, promote stability in client relationships, increase creativity and innovation, and help to foster a more ethical environment.

The added "bonus" is that once this relationship platform is established, then it really gives you the ultimate competitive advantage with your clients; short-term advantages (product, service, price, deliverables, etc.) have no real sustainability. In short, "future proofing" your relationship with the client against competition and market changes.

The perspective I use will be that of the client facing individual(s) or departments within any entity: this could be account managers (key, national, global), brokers, sales representatives (directors, vice presidents, etc.), business development professionals, business owners, marketing managers, brand managers, high level (C band and lower) managers or any person or entity that has external constituents with whom they have to work.. For sake of simplicity. I will call this person's role as "revenue producer" because ultimately they have responsibility for increasing their company's market share and top line.

Before embarking on how to fix the problems, we must know what forces are in play that created the problems in the first place. In that way, we can truly diagnose the disease past the symptoms. Anything less would be ineffectual.

My approach in the presentation of these ideas is to go layer by layer starting with the basic underpinnings of The Honorable Relationship way (philosophy) as it covers why things that were generally acceptable are no longer effective and how to re-think the whole process of selling from the vantage point of the client (as opposed to your point of view).

Chapter 1:
Business NOT As Usual

Patterns in Life

Have you ever wondered why things work the way they do? Or why people act the way they do? If you look at how continents, nations, states, groups, families, and people conduct themselves, you'll start to see that they work in patterns.

Patterns are ingrained in everything we see and do. They drive us whether we are conscious of them or not. The tangible world works in patterns that govern the seasons, weather, animals, and people. The intangible world is also full of patterns. Culture helps to define a lot of patterns that we accept as norms of conduct. We are all creatures of patterns. They have been long established, and as a result they have become almost law-like, seeming to be immutable and unchanging. Patterns can be good (constructive), bad (destructive), or neutral (rare).

The rhythms established early in life are usually built on accepted norms that society allows for the way people conduct themselves. This is true in our personal lives and in our business lives. Understanding the effect of patterns is the first step to realizing their power upon our lives. Patterns are maintained because they are comforting, and offer positive results (such as brushing your teeth each morning and night helps to ward off cavities). Patterns are meant to give stability and structure to one's life, and that is a good thing. However, when external forces change, which renders patterns to be either ineffective or detrimental, then a problem occurs. The problem comes when what we believed to be patterns of effectiveness are no longer that effective. It causes frustration, as these patterns no longer deliver the results that they once had. So sticking to the old, tried and true patterns or methods becomes an exercise in futility.

Just because a large group of people (say a society) believes that these patterns are still valid does not justify keeping these patterns. In fact, these popularly held patterns only make it harder for someone to establish new and more effective patterns of conduct to carry on the business of life or commerce.

There is one main pattern that we will examine in this chapter that most companies adopt which I call: "The Classic Sales Approach" .This pattern has been accepted by the business world and society in general as the way to approach firms, but I contend that it is woefully ineffective in light of major changes that have taken place (See The New Strong Forces in the Business World section later).

Reality Hits Hard

The problem comes from applying outdated and ineffective client management or sales patterns to the rough and tumble environment of today. The results are poor and the consequences are steep:

- In 2007, Pfizer announced that it would be laying off 20% of its sales force. This move was part of a plan to cut costs, after analyzing the success of an often overbearing and always overzealous sales program. Studies recently released indicate that 94% of doctors and medical health professionals feel that drug companies spend far too much in promoting their products. Many hospital and doctors' offices have placed limits not only on the amount of time that doctors will spend with sales reps often down to 90 seconds or less), and are also asking that they stop bringing the pens, pads of paper, tissue boxes, and posters that clutter offices. In addition, over two dozen medical schools are already offering formal classes on how to fend off the sales pitches of Big Pharma, a move that speaks louder than any other sanction about the efficacy of the pharma sales program.[1]

- In 1999, computer giant CompUSA announced it would be releasing half of its commercial sales force – a move that eliminated over 1,800 jobs in one fell swoop. CompUSA reasoned that streamlining their sales force and focusing commercial sales around regional support centers, instead of retail stores, would revive their financial numbers. It never really did.[2]

The Classic Sales Approach

There is a fundamental disconnect between the ingrained, old patterns of sales and/or client management that we all grew up on and the changing environment in which it tries to operate in. The problem lies with the fact that client-facing entities around the world are still operating under methodologies that are very:

- Product Centric

- Technique Focused

- Transaction Based

- Process Oriented

These "classic" methods are very much based on the old sales approaches that still permeate training classes throughout the world. The methods by which to engage clients (customers), how to create business relationships, and how to promote/sell their products are deeply rooted in selling techniques that are decades old.

In order to understand this type of thinking, let's break down the classic sales approach into its component parts:

- Company A's new salesperson is tasked to develop and then sell the most of their product to a prospective account base.

- The salesperson draws from a database or list to solicit. Using this list, that salesperson then proceeds to solicit them using various media: cold calls, mailers, trade show exhibitions, networking, newsletters, etc.

- The sales pitch is usually driven by industry identified needs or product features/benefits. That is to say, the discourse between seller and prospective buyer is on what the salesperson's product can do for the prospective customer in fulfilling their needs.

- The buyer then vets the salesperson's product using various criteria (function, price, timing, terms, etc.) and arrives at a decision to purchase the item(s).

In the process of getting to the last stage, there are some components that the salesperson has employed to try to get to the "buy" stage. In the following rehearsal of these components, I think you will recognize them almost immediately.

Product Centric
(Features/Benefits or Needs/Benefit Driven)

Promoting features and benefits aims to demonstrate to customers why they should choose your product over that of the competition based on the superiority of your product, service, price, or delivery features. This is very ineffective overall as the features that you are currently extolling can be matched or overtaken by the competition.

Focusing on needs and benefits is much more effective in addressing the customer's underlying needs. However, it still lacks depth because the emphasis is on the product rendered and not on the fundamental problems that lie below the requests (addressing symptoms and not diseases). Therefore, it is suspect as to the level of understanding that you may have of the client's needs and their world.

Product-centric selling is inherently flawed due to the fact that you are constantly trying to fit the client's needs into your products or seeing the client only through the prism of your product's capabilities. Therefore, you are trying, perhaps in vain, to make something fit that really doesn't fit. There are cases in which your product/service is not appropriate for the client at all. How can you see that sobering reality when you are only looking at how your product may be used to satisfy clients' needs?

Technique Focused
(Cold Calls, Networking, Closing Techniques)

The techniques that most people employ do have efficacy in various formats. However, what is the underlying premise by which these "tools" are utilized? Tools without a coherent plan for engagement and an overarching long-term strategy may bring results, but not as effectively as when they are guided by a comprehensive plan. A subset of the technique-driven way is the **funnel approach:**

Companies try to amass multiple market targets and apply a sales "blitz" to gain the most amount of "hits". This treats the potential clients as if they were units in a funnel. The main tactic is one of attrition that will sift out the undesirable or unresponsive accounts from the accounts that show promise.

This process is akin to a social phenomenon called speed dating, in which participants go through the process of asking a lot of questions quickly and, based on the answers, a determination is made as to compatibility. This is all about processing large quantities of people and information. But realistically, how can real "fits" be determined under such a scattershot approach? Even if the information gained is accurate, one cannot "hotwire" long-term relationships to move along faster than is readily acceptable or comfortable for the client. Therefore, unless you seek "slam bang" transactions, this model for long-term growth is fallacious. The speed and shallowness of engagement almost guarantees that any outcome is superficial.

An analogy could be made wherein a set of the finest wood-crafting tools was at the disposal of a novice carpenter. These tools would be effective in carrying out a task, but not nearly as useful as they would be in the hands of a master carpenter. Tools without a vision and plan are at best ineffective, and at worst, destructive.

Transaction Based (Having No Long-Term View)

Why are most client approaches not effective in the long run? It is because they usually have two built-in flaws:

- The vision is short term. Companies that view their clients as short-term engagements or are driven by quarter-to-quarter results simply do not see the process of client work as being a multi-year endeavor, the fruits of which increase with time.

- Client relations are transaction driven. The function of filling a client's needs becomes the glue that binds the vendor to the client, and that is essentially all that is there. While these relationships may be amicable or even friendly, the relationships have no depth or foothold other than transactional. Hence, when stormy weather hits or (even worse) when there are others that could fulfill the transactions in a more beneficial manner, these already weak bonds become easily severable.

This truly is the Achilles heel of a lot of client-facing methodologies. If you review all that you have read, experienced and absorbed regarding sales, you will find that the foundation of almost all its teachings is based on transaction-focused thinking. Like a solid, wonderfully built house on a poorly laid foundation, no matter how great the construction of the upper levels, if the base is substandard, then the results can only be disastrous.

Subservient Collaboration (Process Oriented)

A lot of selling companies have adopted the policy of working through the buyer's procurement policies to the letter (no dialogue, electronic interface, etc.). Conformance to these various procurement rules as sole method of conducting business without any true interaction or building of relationships will significantly shift the balance of power to the buying company, which is not a good thing. What that does is to set up a master/servant relationship between buyer and seller, respectively, in which the seller is very much dependent on conformity to buyer's rules with little or no input.

This process may make the buyer's procurement departments happy but it is deleterious to the selling company's agendas and true participation in the transaction. This process-oriented thinking in which the seller dances to the tune that the buyer plays is not conducive to true partnering and sets a pattern of subservience that may continue and expand into other aspects of the buyer/ seller relationship.

An extreme example of this subservience taken to new heights (or lows, I guess) is the reverse auction bid. For those that are uninitiated into this terrible bidding device, here are the ground rules:

- The buyer invites competing seller companies to an electronic auction wherein none of the competitors/bidders know any of the other participants' identity BUT they do see the competing bids.

- When the commencement of the bidding begins, there is an allotted time for the bids. As you bid, you can also see competing bids.

- It is very much like a conventional bid except for one notable exception – the prices that are bid go DOWN, not up! Hence the name: reverse auction bid.

- When the bidding time has expired, the buyer can see who was the lowest pricing of various aspects of the bid.

The insidious thing about such an auction, even with all the caveats that pricing is not the final determinant of winning the bid, is that the sellers slavishly lower their own pricing to a level that may be acceptable to the buyer (or may not) with NO consideration of anything but pricing levels. This process is sheer folly for selling companies with any level of integrity and reputation and yet it is surprising the numbers of companies that participate. Why? Because that is the way to get the coveted buyer's business.

The Enablers of the Problem

The natural question is then: why do people still do these things if they are not very effective? There are several factors which help to perpetuate this "classic" type of approach. The following are the main reasons:

- It is what we are familiar with. We've been taught from early on that the approach of "classical" sales is what really works. For some, it may have started from selling cookies or candy to raise funds for school trips or summer camp. Some learned it through work. In whatever form it was disseminated, the approach was promulgated as the way to go.

- Vast numbers of people using it. Like most things in life, the more people who adopt a way of thinking, the more it becomes a fact or normative standard. Just because it is accepted en masse does not ensure its validity (NOTE: Remember "flat earth" thinking by the ancients?).

- There is nothing really to replace the "classic" client approach. What is in the marketplace that has effectively taken its place? There are variants of sales based on techniques but they are all very mechanistic and still lack the true glue that binds people and organizations together.

- It works! If it didn't work, no one would use it. Obviously the "classic" client approach has efficacy but the technique is becoming less effective due to overwhelming competition. However, up until a clear line of demarcation, the "classic" client approach does truly work. In fact, it seems well suited for certain industries and products, which are usually lower priced, less risk bearing, and volume based.

When the Classic Sales Approach Works Best

So as not to misrepresent, I can personally see the efficacy of the classic sales method under certain conditions. The following situations are when this approach is most effective:

- The product has a low price or risk threshold.

- The product is fairly uncomplicated.

- The level of commitment by the buyer is very low in terms of time, effort, and cost.

Toothpicks, toilet paper, or basic products like these would definitely fall into the aforementioned listing for types of purchasing decisions that would be conducive to "classic" client approach.

These older models for client engagement would probably continue to work except that there are forces that have come into being and gathered strength in the recent past that have effectively nullified much of the strengths of the classic model.

Some of these major global forces have come into existence linked and some have come to the fore by themselves. It doesn't much matter, for our purposes, how they came about, suffice to say that they are here to stay on an indefinite timeline.

Case Citing – An Interesting Paradox:

A conundrum occurs as you go up higher in the food chain of buying decisions. Have you noticed that car sales and home sales are also conducted using the "classic" method? This apparently negates the first characteristics of when the "classic" client approach works best which is when the product has a low price or risk threshold. As we all know, the purchase of a car and home represents the two largest types of purchases that most people will ever make. Yet, how is it that these large dollar and fairly "risky" purchases respond positively to the classic model?

Upon a deeper look, the apparent disconnection is resolved when you consider one other factor. The decision to buy a car or a home is usually confined to the purchaser and his immediate family in terms of felt consequences. No one at work would know (unless told) about the "lemon" car or "money pit" house that you purchased. Only you feel the full consequences of a bad decision.

A bad decision in the purchase of car or home is <u>not</u> something that will influence the direction of your job or career. As a result, the "classic" approach still works because, while the stakes are high personally, they are non-existent professionally.

Chapter 2:
The New Strong Forces in the Business World

The new strong forces in the business world did not happen overnight. They came as the latest iteration of what the business world has developed in reaction to technological, societal, and political changes. Most of us would be able to identify a lot of these trends as laid out below; however, have we really incorporated them into how we live and do business? If not, then we may consider their long-range effects because they have affected the way we conduct business by creating the volatile and cutthroat environment we find ourselves in today.

I have listed 12 strong forces and they byproducts of them. There may be more but, for our discussion purposes, this list will suffice.

Commoditization

We've all seen this happen. The rate of its acceptance and promulgation is only accelerating with each passing day. Commoditization occurs when businesses and organizations treat employees, vendors, clients, or any other party as indistinguishable units. It is the natural extension of mass production methodologies and it is now becoming the operative standard for looking at people, services, products, talents, skills, and companies. The basic premise is that each of us is a quantifiable and fairly homogenous unit in whatever market segment we occupy.

An article in Al Bawaba News details the dilemma currently facing telecom operators worldwide. As the complexity of the telecommunications industry continues to deepen, the focus of operators has drifted away from customer service to maintaining operations. Leaders in the field are actually suggesting outsourcing network functions to allow telecom operators to focus on the most important part of their business — client interface and personal attention.[3]

Example: Let's use an example of a basic product maker such as a basket company and the customers of this basket making company.

A corporate buyer of baskets may quantify baskets by shape, size, style, manufacturing origin, and price. Any slight deviations may be factored in, but generally this view seeks to quantify the baskets into "known" elements to be judged and compared. The goal is to "gentrify" the basket product so that it becomes more predictable to procure, handle, and re-sell or use.

In looking at people, products, and companies this way, the basket buyer will also create systems and methods to reduce wide variations and discrepancies.

Byproducts:

RFP (Request for Proposals) – A **Request for Proposal** is a request for suppliers to create a proposal regarding a specific product (or service) through a bidding process with procurement or sourcing departments. A study recently found that RFPs typically cost anywhere from $50,000 to $250,000 to complete. More disturbing is the fact that only one third of completed RFPs result in actual implementation – meaning that RFPs create an enormous amount of wasted time effort, and money. [4]

Procurement or Sourcing Departments – Procurement departments were created to get maximum "value" for minimum cost/expense for companies.

KPI (Key Performance Indicators) – **Key Performance Indicators**, or business activity monitoring, are metrics based on financial and non-financial information that reflects the performance of an organization, or an individual within an organization. **Credit Union Magazine** published an article in their February 2007 edition which remarked that KPIs are not only based on metrics that are irrelevant to individual members of a corporate community, but also function to keep people focused on past performance instead of working towards future goals. [5]

SLAs (Service Level Agreements) – A Service Level Agreement is a contract that defines the level of service, priorities, responsibilities, and other factors between customers and service providers. While the main purpose is supposed to focus on defining the level of service expected, it is often used mostly as a punitive device if objectives are not met.

Reverse Auction Bids – A **Reverse Auction**, as the title suggests, is a situation where sellers compete to give the lowest price for their services to a buyer through an anonymous bidding electronic vehicle. Its ultimate goal is to give the buyer a demonstrable indication of how low in pricing the various parties are willing to go.

Compartmentalization

Compartmentalization puts businesses and people into a "box", literally. There is a push for one official point of contact through which anyone can interact with a business or organization.

This is tends to be the procurement or sourcing division of a company. Once again, the driving force is to create stability of input/output for communication and relations.

Example: The basket-buying company (using the previous example) limits the level, type and frequency of interactions between its other departments and the basket sellers. The goal is to have the business relationship managed through one department, and any interactions between the basket-selling company and other departments or divisions of the basket buyer is highly discouraged.

What comes of this? It can cause pre-definition of what the basket buyer wants without giving any latitude to be creative or innovative on the part of the basket seller. Consider this: if you have one procurement person be the driver in making decisions as to what will and will not be purchased, then how good can they be in picking up on the nuances of products as diverse as financial services, operating machinery, security systems, ERP (enterprise resource programs), etc.? Even if you inject the input of the vested party into the process such as the finance department, operations, security department, etc., do you really get a decision predicated on the "best" mix of product, price and effectiveness? Or rather, in the case of many situations, do procurement departments tend to dominate the process so much so that purchasing decisions are made that counter the desired outcomes and decisions of the original stakeholder department that is ultimately the user of these products? (See Procurement-Based Thinking later)

Byproducts:

Task Driven Actions – Being task driven occurs when individuals, organizations, or companies make decisions based on short-term goals instead of long-term vision.

Poor Communication – Bad or ineffective communication occurs when business partners, clients, and suppliers are not allowed to discuss openly issues that affect production or supply. This fosters bad decisions and results.

Lack of Transparency – When there is lack of transparency between two parties (buyer and seller), then there is a severely limiting, artificial imposition that prevents innovation and creativity in solving problems that may exist in the client/vendor relationship or organization.

Subordinate Relationships – This type of relationship is really not optimal for anyone contrary to what some people may think. When there is master/servant situation, what happens is usually abuse of the weaker party (which is not tenable in the long run).

Systemization

As the world becomes more complex, there is an increased reliance on systems for handling, such as procurement, provisioning, and vendor management. With this reliance comes programmatic thinking and impersonal transactions. A prime example of the downfall of over-systemization can be found in the *Modernising Medical Careers* program that has been implemented throughout England to regulate the posting of doctors. Both patients and physicians have been adversely affected by this program, which places doctors, without regard to their personal needs or those of their patients, at posts only based on the local need and not the doctor's specialty, talents, or career goals. Patients get inadequate care from doctors that are either frustrated or overburdened by a mechanical system that has no "human" input.[6]

The importance of personal contact and face-to-face communication cannot be overstated. For decades, the value of interpersonal relations has been touted, and studies demonstrating that over two-thirds of communication is achieved through body language only serve to further prove this point.[7]

Problems faced by records management professionals globally also reflect the negative impact of over-systemization. Using technology alone to make decisions regarding records management (or any field, for that matter) often results in wasted time and capital spent adapting to a new system that is implemented simply to improve the productivity that it disrupts.[8]

Example: The basket seller must adhere to a procurement system (usually automated) that will place orders by quantity, style, size, price, and other previously determined attributes. Due to the automatic nature of these orders, the "face" time between the basket buyer and seller is severely limited.

Byproducts:

Lack of Human Involvement – More and more often, businesses are choosing the path of technological rather than human involvement. Classic processes (sales, requisitioning, and implementation) become rote, driven by algorithms instead of by human judgment. There is less reliance on the intuitive nature of the human decision-making process with proponents of these systems arguing that such systemizations create a more empirically objective (i.e., balanced) way of managing business relations.

Over-Reliance on Technology – Many companies unfortunately become over-reliant on technology as more and more transactions are conducted either between two machines, or between a person and a machine instead of through human interaction.

Constriction – As factors in decision-making are continually reduced to mere factors in an algorithm, any decisions not readily quantifiable will become greatly slowed.

One-Stop-Shopping

Another trend promotes one or a limited number of vendors who have the capability to offer a full suite of services over companies that offer individual or a limited number of services. This reduces the need to have a multiplicity of vendors and creates more reliance on key providers who are called to serve in different capacities and areas.

Many companies have been taking this route, integrating more services and offerings into their product lines in order to attract more business. A prime example would be Microsoft's acquisition of aQuantive, expanding its digital marketing reach to match that of major competitors such as Google and Yahoo. In many cases, this move towards one-stop-shopping is not simply viewed as a business decision – it is deemed necessary for the survival of the company at large.[9]

While it seems at face value to be a positive step for companies ready to 'take the plunge' into expanding offerings, over-integration has a dark side that must be acknowledged. The San Diego State University Library experienced just such an array of problems while trying to create a one-stop-atmosphere in a University library. While their changes were well-intentioned and looked excellent on paper, their wider offering of services not only made the libraries more difficult to navigate both physically and technologically, they created far more problems than they solved for students and professors who were trying to conduct research, (which had the possibility to increase the prestige of the University as a whole).[10]

> *Example: The basket seller may present the company as not only producers of baskets but also as being capable of helping to design, finance, and produce a line solely for the buyer (on a subcontracted basis). The basket seller could help to train or consult the basket-buying company's employees on the latest technology or information in that industry. Perhaps the engineering department of the basket seller could help to solve sourcing problems that the buyer may have.*

Byproducts:

Success of Integrators – Companies that are able to successfully integrate a variety of services related to their industry are able to meet increasingly complex customer needs.

Need for Continuity – Companies develop an unnecessary need for continuity, wherein they become overly reliant on homogenous pools of talent and suppliers, stifling some venues for creativity and innovation.

Complex Solutions – In order to solve complex problems, equally complex solutions must be developed. This often creates different problems instead of solving them. This results in the development of a distaste to "vet" other vendors

Off shoring to the Global Marketplace

In the modern business world, companies are constantly pushing outside of known markets and into less known or foreign markets searching for competitive advantages in price, services, and logistics either in the creation or selling of their products or services.

While everyone is familiar with the more visible results of off shoring such as the loss of jobs nationally and decreased capital investment at home, there are many other areas where off shoring has had a deep impact. An article by Michael Mandel of BusinessWeek August 2007 noted the sometimes extreme lengths employees have to go to in order to remain valuable to a company – such as the growing "mobile workforce" in Europe that travels extensively in order to retain their positions and avoid being "off shored".[11]

Example: The basket buyer may seek to look at other markets not only for better pricing (perhaps the baskets are made more cheaply in foreign markets) but also more variety drawing from indigenous culture art and baskets to inspire new lines.

Byproducts:

Rigorous Competition – As new markets are entered, new competitors are both discovered and rated through the introduction of new products, technology, and partnership opportunities. There is also increased pressure to reduce prices and increase performance as more players enter markets.

Fewer Boundaries (Effort, Time, Cost) in Traversing National Borders – As technology allows companies to communicate more quickly and effectively, the expansion of business into the global marketplace is greatly enhanced by fewer boundaries despite physical distance.

The Leveling Effect – Global markets are putting pressure on companies to reduce prices while simultaneously increasing performance, which can lead to difficulties in maintaining sustainability as a business entity.

Generic Markets and Processes – As cultural boundaries are routinely crossed, there is a greater call for "gentrification" of products. Businesses, in turn, mirror this trend by pushing for a more homogenous market that allows for the same processes to be applied across continents.

Increased Uncertainty – Any new market creates uncertainty and unease, and the added instability of many countries in which companies are pushing to do business only serves to further destabilize the security of global markets.

Disposability

More and more often, there is a tendency towards businesses having quick and immediate disconnections with their business partners. Whether it is for purposes of liability or efficiency, businesses seek non-binding contracts and relationships which can be severed quickly. Because of this, business relationships tend to be need and performance-driven and are temporal in nature.

A study by Vantage Partners recently showed that 65% to 70% of strategic business partnerships are doomed to failure – a fact which Adrian Mello of Electronic Business says is exacerbated by the tendency of executives to choose partners and partnership structures that are "in vogue" (such as joint ventures) instead of choosing a partnership that is best for the company.[12]

One of the most fabulously capital-draining failed partnerships of 2001 was between AT&T and British Telecommunications, a venture called "Concert". The program (which was supposed to provide global communication services) resulted in a loss of almost $200,000,000 per quarter because of failed attempts to achieve a successful synergy. This is a very costly example of the results of partners not being focused on making a relationship work effectively to achieve common goals.[13]

Example: The basket-buying company may feel that there are no backups if their main basket-selling (vending) company were to have production issues or not offer market competitive styling or pricing. To counter this over reliance, the basket-buying company looks to multiple vendors that are able to fill layers of needs.

Byproducts:

Shorter Contractual Relationships – As the incidents of longstanding relationships diminish, relationships become contractually based and much shorter in nature.

More Turnover in Relationships (Churning) – A great turnover of business relationships occurs, decreasing effectiveness by requiring new systems and partnerships to be learned and then unlearned.

More Instability – This causes instability not only within the business engaged in these short-term relationships, but also in the markets they inhabit.

More Lawsuits – As lack of trust and carefully structured liability clauses continue to escalate in use, the incidents of lawsuits are only poised to increase.

Increasing Complexity

In today's business world, complexity is increasing at a very high rate of speed. Caused by iterations in markets and technology, there is greater demand for more complex solutions than previously offered.

Example: The basket-buying company may require the basket seller to provide their product on a JIT (just-in-time) basis, keep inventory and trend analysis information, offer logistics packaging for delivery of the goods, carry or extend credit to the buyer, etc.

Byproducts:

Holistic Thinking – Clients require more holistic thinking, which encompasses more than a simple needs-solution-based business partnership.

Guidance – More than a simple vendor-buyer relationship, clients often require guidance from their suppliers. This requires companies to act more like business partners than simply as a selling agency.

Credibility and Trust – Many clients require credibility and trust from their business partners in order to have a functioning business relationship.

Client Knowledge – Companies can no longer simply rely on their knowledge of a market to get business. They must also develop extensive client knowledge in order to be truly competitive in today's environment.

Increasing Concerns about Liability and Compliance

Today, more contracts have mitigating or risk containment wording which seeks to shift the risk and liability of the business to their partners. These contracts invariably contain disclosure restrictions, competitive prohibitions, service level agreements (SLAs), severability, termination clauses, indemnification provisions, etc. These are all designed to favor the stronger party of the relationship (usually the buyer).

Example: The basket buyer creates a contract that effectively shifts the cost of litigation and damages that may come from faulty or inferior workmanship to their basket-selling vendor partners. The buyer also acknowledges little if any responsibility to potentially offended parties.

Byproducts:

Litigation – Because of the transparency and fast communication requisite of the modern business world, incidents of litigation are becoming more and more frequent as companies take unethical actions in order to achieve a goal, and are far more likely to be caught (and punished) than in the past.

Hidden Costs – As doing business and remaining compliant with the many clauses of contracts today continues to increase in complexity, many hidden costs are accrued by all parties involved in business partnerships in order to assure that business is being conducted with integrity.

Call for Stability – As patterns and groundwork continue to change in global business, companies find themselves clamoring for assurances of stability, either written into contracts (as described above) or by changing their own business practices.

Increased Turnover – As relationships continue to grow weaker (no longer based on solid principles that ensure longevity), fewer relationships will survive to prosper and increase revenue for both sellers and buyers.

Outsourcing

Many of today's business leaders feel a need to have others do the "work" of ancillary (and even core) functions. As the cost of doing business continues to rise, companies try to amend their budgets by handing off the work to external firms who can complete the task at a much lower expense, thereby decreasing their own overhead.

Example: The basket-buying company is outsourcing its functions such as procurement, manufacturing, logistics, human resource, etc. to lower costs of doing business. This creates an army of facilitators that do the bidding of their client but do not have true allegiance or knowledge of the client and their agenda.

Byproducts:

Outside Help – As outsourcing continues to grow more common, the comfort level that management has with passing off tasks to outsiders continues to increase.

Valuable Partners – In searching for the perfect firm to outsource to, it has become more and more important for companies to find companies that can add great "value" for clients requiring outsourcing services.

Cultural Barriers - When coupled with off shoring, outsourcing can lead to problems such as cultural differences and increased costs related to conducting business internationally.

Resource Challenged, not Budget Challenged

Distaste for adding more internal staff presents challenges in getting all internal functions accomplished or covered. Hence the need for outside augmentation, whenever possible, to offset the pressing needs of the business is more attractive than hiring permanent internal staffing with its attendant and recurring costs.

Example: The basket-buying company may be willing to hire "temporary" or "transitory" talent from augmentation companies to cover pressing business functions. The irony is that while the basket-buying company is willing to spend for augmentation, they are not willing to devote resources for the hiring of permanent internal staff.

Byproducts:

Augmentation - In order to fill semi-permanent gaps, more augmentation is pursued by companies looking to keep costs low.

Increased Projects - More resources are being devoted to complete tasks on a project basis, instead of working towards long-term, unified goals.

Increased Volatility – A lack of continuity internally promotes volatility while diminishing the focus on a coherent, sustainable strategy.

Project Management Thinking

What started out as a practical way of getting things done in a business setting has morphed into a whole way of thinking and processing information. Spurred by the popularity of consultants, project management has evolved as a prominent way of thinking. Project management is when people and resources are drawn together for a very finite period of time to work on a main task. The effectiveness of this very powerful tool cannot be disputed, but the wholesale adoption of this thinking (fueled by the ever shortening tenure of company leadership) is disturbing. The concern is that well-executed projects may not mesh with each other and may be promulgated due to individual business unit's goals but not with the overall company's goals in mind.

Example: The basket-selling company is working on several projects to enhance its basket-based products by drawing from the skill and expertise of the company's internal and external resources. It will be difficult to keep all the parties coordinated and moving forward. Also, there is an added challenge of coherency as these projects take on a "life of their own" in terms of sub-projects and the need for perpetuation.

Byproducts:

"Silo" Thinking - Disjointed and disconnected teams that begin to move forward (at first amicably) but which may later be at odds due to resource or budgetary allocations

Self-Perpetuation Dynamics - The need to keep some projects going even though their main purpose is no longer as valued except as part of a political agenda

"Rabbit" Trails Syndrome – Various side projects and initiatives that may spring up during typical project work

Lack of Overall Vision – The increasing difficulty to retain coherency of vision for the overall plan that comes from multiple projects deployed at the same time

Procurement-Based Thinking

Many companies have created a corps of professional "procurers" whose sole raison d'etre is to acquire products and services for the firm. The idea stems from applying a disciplined management template to the buying or acquisition process, thereby creating a measurable format. However, due to the complexity and multiplicity of products and services, as well as industrial, cultural, or regional differences, these procurement managers are sometimes woefully uneducated in applying the buying decision templates to their selection criteria. This can even be a problem with the added support and knowledge of the department that is actually requesting and paying for the product or service (vested party).

> *Example: The basket-buying company is interested in "native" baskets from around the world (as part of their international line of baskets). They have asked their procurement team to source bids from various countries in Southeast Asian, Latin American, and African locations. Due to the complexity of the materials, the type of volume levels, local taxes and regulations, and the quality of workmanship, the procurement department needs to expand their criteria categories along with re-defining some of their mainstay criteria such as "quality", "timeliness", etc.*

Byproducts:

Lack of Knowledge in the Discipline or Industry – While it is a great tool for standardization, uniformity, and control, procurement departments cannot possibly be expected to be knowledgeable about every widget, gadget, discipline, industry, and area that exists. This gap of knowledge can lead to very "correct" decisions that are bad ones nonetheless.

Homogeneity of Decisions and Outcomes - This templated approach, while more logical, is also (let's face it) normative and boring. That is the main purpose of the exercise of procurement – to weed out aberrant or extreme types of decisions. Procurement departments work on the paradigm of "minimum thresholds" or "lowest common denominators." That is what they do best. But is that the best for the company?

Mistaking "Price" for "Value" – We will cover this later in the book, but suffice to say that many, many people make the mistake that they got great "value" by getting something for the lowest "price". What is missing is the concept and reality of "use value", which will be discussed later.

In delineating these "12 Strong Forces in the Business World", you can probably see other trends in today's marketplace that are offshoots of these main themes. These trends have real consequences. With their power and ascension in the hierarchy of global trends grows, they are the new "realities" of doing business in the 21st century (at least in the foreseeable future).

Chapter 3:
The Effects of the Strong Forces

The reason that the 12 Strong Forces came into being is as a result of the buyers' side trying to be more efficient and cost-effective. Those are enviable goals to pursue and achieve at any period or any cultural setting. However, man being man, we are never satisfied with status quo. The standard is always lifted as one company or group seeks to out-do the other in terms of these sought-after efficiencies and cost savings.

As a result of hiring very smart, sharp consultants to raise the bar for themselves, these buying companies (who tend to be the monoliths of their respective industries) have put into place systems, methodologies, and practices that purposely create a less level playing field. The ultimate goal is to create a market advantage that tilts as much of the odds toward the buying company as much as possible.

The consequences of these changes, brought upon by these very large buying companies, DO NOT favor the selling companies or channel partners to these behemoths. Look back at the list of the 12 Strong Forces and their residual effects. Do you see at a high level what they are doing to the buying/selling landscape? Here are some obvious consequences:

Watering Down of Uniqueness

Unless you establish a certain uniqueness, reputation or brand, most selling companies will be relegated to the heap called "generic" which is what the trend of commoditization has done. The classic client approach of features/benefit or needs/benefit is by nature product centric in thinking. Having said that, then the trend towards commoditization by the world's business markets will only lessen the impact of how your product/service may be distinctive or better than others. A classic case of world changing technology reduced to a commodity is highlighted in Case Citing: What happens when cutting edge becomes boring in Chapter 7 later.

Procurement-based thinking also has a neutralizing effect on product-based thinking because procurement departments look at everything in terms of price, features, time, and deliverables. The need to turn things into "units" runs high in this way of doing business. This approach, along with Offshoring to Global Marketplace, makes any product reproducible at lower price points and thereby reduces the impact of selling companies' products.

Control of Dialogue and Access

When people or companies are not able to communicate due to Compartmentalization or Systemization trends, then what happens is that some have all the advantages and most do not. As a result of this dictum, the oversized buyer usually holds most of the advantage because they have one point of contact to face the world or they have systems to buffer their company from the onslaught of vendors. While that may seem bad to everyone except the buyer, in actuality the buyer is also disadvantaged by such an environment. The buyer doesn't benefit from the very necessary real-time information exchanges when there are barriers for selling companies to talk to the vested members of the buying companies. Innovation is also crippled due to these artificial constraints.

In light of these restrictions, what happens is that classic sales approaches that are Technique Focused such as cold calling, networking, etc. become less effective because these are specifically why the control of dialogue was put into place – to reduce discussions and access.

Adding More Links to the Chain Between Ultimate Seller and Buyer

The more links you add to any chain (whether it be people, parties, or processes) that connect the seller and buyer together, the harder it is to have direct, effective and simple communication and execution.

Procurement-based thinking, along with Global Offshoring and Outsourcing, add more links to the chain and thereby make access to the true decision makers harder and harder. While this may not be the original or sole reason why these forces came into being, nonetheless the result is that they shield decision makers behind a curtain of people and processes so as to keep them from being pestered by sales and to give them anonymity until the choice has been made. This may be a cynical viewpoint but from the selling company's view, that is exactly what buying companies do.

When the communication/execution chain lengthens (in any relationship), then the relationship becomes: overly complex, less personal and familiar, and more tenuous. They are easily severable.

So a decision needs to be reached by selling companies: do you want to continue completing RFPs and working with procurement people exclusively (which fosters Subservient Collaboration) or do you want to increase your chances of successfully bidding for the business, because to do these tasks without entrée into higher level decision making will basically condemn the selling firms to a subservient role.

Making Things More Complex and Yet More Dumbed Down

As matters become more complex and businesses are requiring more from their vending partners, the burden is on the selling companies to match the ever increasing expectations. Forces such as One Stop Shopping, Overall Increased Complexity, and Emphasis on Liability and Compliance make doing business with these buying firms more difficult because the standard product-driven answers are no longer acceptable. Indeed, these forces have made the days of just offering one set of products or services to fill a niche no longer adequate.

Nowadays, firms must solve problems or increase productivity of their buying partners in order to make the buyer's world easier (more simplified). Companies with product centric focus or that have transaction-based models are finding that their inwardly looking paradigms have a blind spot. That blind spot is <u>that they are not looking at their interactions (or relationship) with the client as their real "product" or strength</u>. For example, if you make shelving for a big box retailer, you will probably be asked to address issues such as logistics (storing, transportation, records management), financing (credit terms/plans), advertising (end cap displays, media spending), etc. Clients or buying companies are seeking simple answers to very complex problems from the companies that sell to them. This has been beyond the pale of what traditional product-centric firms can do for their clients.

So what is the poor basket selling company (in the examples given) to do as it faces this tsunami wave of influences? It seems that traditional approaches that are product centric, transaction based, technique focused and process oriented are losing momentum in the emerging business world.

What is a way to counteract these events and trends so as to tip the balance to the selling company's side?

Chapter 4:
Template for Success

This chapter lays out what will work to solve the problems that the modern marketplace presents to those who are selling. With all successful relationships, be it personal or business, the main ingredients and their sequence are critical. Think back as to how you first became friends with your best friend or how you got to know and later marry your spouse or how you have gotten into a great business relationship with your best client. If you trace back the threads, I think you will find that the commonality for all these relationships is exemplified in the flowchart shown:

Knowledge → Understanding Use Value →Relationships →Exploration

The progression of how two strangers become friends, lovers, or business associates tracks the same way whether the vested parties are aware of it or not. This cascading flow diagram shows how good relationships foster seamless transition from one strength to another one.

1. **Knowledge** of each other in terms of strengths, weaknesses, capabilities, world views, and work/personal style and conduct is the starting point of the relationship. This tentative information reconnaissance is critical in the formation of a strong relationship platform. It is the beginning building block of a solidly built partnership. How is that mutual knowledge gained? By finding out more about that person and their world, of course. By doing your homework as it were. And by knowing yourself and your strengths/weaknesses and likes/dislikes. That's how you get to go from strangers with no visible points of accord and commonality to acquaintances.

2. **Understanding Use Value** comes from knowledge of each other. Use value is the valuation of the uses that may come of this business/ personal collaboration, the value of which is much more dependent on the "hidden" uses as much as outwardly appearing uses. Use values may be more rooted in emotional, financial, strategic, political, operational motives than just superficial physical aspects of the product/service/

company. These use values are the underpinnings from which a strong relationship is further developed because, beyond all the talk of "synergy" and "a true partnership", there are no truly "altruistic" relationships. Almost all of them are based on uses that may be derived from the relationships.

Understanding use value in a personal relationship comes from the knowledge and information gleaned from the "Knowledge" step delineated above and how the other person's character, attributes, style, etc. may fit into your world. If there are more or compelling use values derived from a person's level of affection, ability to communicate and relate, and, for spouses, how they may be able to support oneself through the balance of a life (financially, emotionally, physically, spiritually), then chances are very good that you proceed past acquaintance level.

The dynamic for business is the same, only not as intimate. Or is it? I've seen business relationships that are very close (not sexual) and just as demanding/uplifting as personal ones.

NOTE: I know that it may sound Machiavellian to talk about use value as it pertains to personal relations and in no way am I denigrating the human race by classifying us as "consumers" with personal, emotional use value radar looking for people to fulfill all their units of use values. However, I think it is fair to say that people are not altruistic in nature and do form bonds that come from filling needs that they are seeking to fulfill. If you doubt that, then simply look at the Personal Classified ads in any newspaper or online dating service sites.

3. **Relationships** develop with time and positive experiences that would never have happened had there not been the exploratory, knowledge-seeking venture first and the realization that there are definite positive "uses" to having and promoting this relationship. The next step is the furtherance of these relationships by testing them via experience and time. The more time that has passed and experiences that have been shared with a beginning relationship, then the more the relationship (friend, love, business associate) matures. Like learning to dance with a new partner, with every new day the partners learn from each other as to how to move and interact. If, while doing the relationship dance, either

one or both parties find that there are more "left feet" incidents than smooth ballroom sweeps, then the relationship may either cool or end. Relationships that are built and forged carefully in the heat of business are not accidents. They take time and care to provide the benefits derived thereof from all vested parties. There is a lot of deliberation and work involved.

The net effect from this phase is a strong foundation of friendship, marriage (if personal) or true partnering in the business lexicon. But wait there's more....

4. **Exploration** comes from the trust and credibility that was established by the strong personal/working relationships. Trust is the platform from which there is a genuine willingness to take a healthy amount of risk and explore new avenues or possibilities. These possibilities could include moving to another part of the world or career changes (if personal). Or it could be new innovations or radical new approaches in business. But why would anyone take such risks? Because the battle-tested relationship was able to show the participants for what they truly are: competent and honorable entities that can cover each other's back in times of need or stress. Therefore, there is more of a willingness to go into uncharted territories with their battle-tested comrade than with untested people or entities.

   This is the zenith of any relationship, whether it be personal or business. Not to belabor the point but, if the aforementioned stages were ones of courtship between a man and woman, then this phase is one where the couple is married, have three kids and are working on a house renovation! Talk about trust!!

Each step, (knowledge, understanding use value, relationship, and exploration) cascades into the next, and the net effect is an environment that promotes growth and responsible risk taking. This is the way it used to work and the way it should work. This is the way it STILL works if we don't stifle these natural tendencies with artificially constricting devices.

So, now we have a master blueprint of how we are going to re-engineer your business and how it is to be conducted. Let's get into the details of how to move forward.

Chapter 5:
Know Thyself:
Seeing Things in a Different Way

"Know thyself" is a very famous quote attributed to Socrates. I think it epitomizes what one must do in order to be successful in the client management and selling world. An honest self-assessment is key to ending bad patterns and establishing and maintaining good ones. The first important task is to establish what it is that you and your company really have to offer in the marketplace.

Define What You Are Really Selling or How You See the Product

People love to state that the customer is best served when you sell the product that brings them "value". Stated in another way, people seek value in what is bought. This amorphous "value" and the perception of it in a product is the final determinant of what is purchased and at what quantities and at what prices.

But what is "value"? And how is it determined? NOTE: We will cover "use value", which is what people really mean when they say the word "value", later.

Some may proffer other ideas and formulas and ways of quantifying this ephemeral factor called "value" but, in the end, it is an exercise in futility especially as it almost invariably has a component that is very subjective such as accuracy, quality, timeliness, etc. and the weighting thereof.

But we can't give up this investigation because to be successful in uncovering the client's intrinsic needs and what he/she values can yield great rewards. So let's look at why people buy what they actually buy. Almost always, people acquire things because it serves a need or want, whether real or perceived. So, in order to sell something at a price that works for both seller and buyer, the seller must understand what it is that is motivating potential clients to buy the product. Yes, at first the decision to purchase is usually based on logical, rational, and defensible thinking. However, the tipping point of whether to buy/not buy from one seller of product or services versus another seller is not as easily quantifiable or logical.

To understand the reason why one seller's product is chosen over someone else's is essential in moving forward with your clients. The spotlight must now be focused on a deceptively simple question....what are you really selling to the client?

If you say the product, you are missing the mark. If you cite your product's or service's features and benefits, you are still missing the point. Why is that? Because you are concentrating on your product, your features, your benefits, and your view of the world.

Remember, that's how the classic sales model operates, and while it has efficacy to a certain level, it fails more often than it succeeds because the emphasis is on everything except the most important thing – the client and the use value he/she derives from the product/service. In order to free ourselves of this calcified thinking then, we must divest ourselves of product centric thinking. This means that we must not concentrate on our product, our company or ourselves but what are the fundamental needs and wants of the client that yearn to be fulfilled to begin with.

How should one perceive what they have to offer? Here's a hint. **For those who can see their product not as a product but as a vehicle or delivery mechanism of what the client wants, then they are on the right track for successful long-term relationships.** Because ultimately, this type of perception and reaction to the knowledge of the client is what will prevent obsolescence – now and in the future.

It is all about what the customer wants to achieve and accomplish and how your "product" can fulfill those use values. There are some companies and some people that "get it". They understand this concept and they execute accordingly. But much like one of those pointillistic paintings in which you at first see a field of different colored dots but when you relax and focus on the painting, then you see a totally different and coherent picture "submerged" underneath the overtly noticeable dots. The surprising thing is that it was there all the time but only with the right frame of mind/sight are you able to "see" the image underlying the chaotic dots of the picture. In a way, that's what you have to do to get to this level.

A quick way to illustrate this point is the following exercise:

What do these companies make and sell?

Companies	What They Sell
Toyota, Ford, Lexus, Nissan	Cars
Hilton, Marriott, Hyatt, Sheraton	Hotel rooms
Barnes & Noble, Borders	Books, magazines, information
Wal-Mart, Home Depot, Amazon.com, Best Buy	Grocery items, books, electronics, clothing, etc.
Starbucks, Seattle's Best Coffee, Tully's	Coffee
Federal Express, DHL, UPS	Letters & packages being moved quickly
Apple (iPod, iTunes, iPhones, iMac)	Computers, phones, entertainment

At first look, the answers seem correct because that is what these companies physically build, offer and sell. However, look at the same list of companies under a different perspective and you will see how the answers will lead you to think differently.

What do these companies make and sell?

Companies	What They Sell
Toyota, Ford, Lexus, Nissan	Transportation that creates an environment of safety, luxury, convenience, etc.
Hilton, Marriott, Hyatt, Sheraton	A safe, clean, comfortable room and a good night's sleep
Barnes & Noble, Borders	A place to sit and read, to use as a resource. A type of private library
Wal-Mart, Home Depot, Amazon.com, Best Buy	One-stop shopping, convenience, volume pricing
Starbucks, Seattle's Best Coffee, Tully's	A lifestyle, café society, a place to socialize or work
Federal Express, DHL, UPS	Speed, dependability, business facilitators
Apple (iPod, iTunes, iPhones, iMac)	A lifestyle, design, innovation, specialization, chic, social causes

What is the difference? The difference is the first view is very product oriented (the physical uses derived from these products) whereas the second view is more of what the customers (clients) view as the real "product" or use value derived from these products (or at least how they perceive the use values that these products offer to them in their lives).

When you look at your product as a vehicle or medium by which to fulfill a market's use value, then you begin to think of your product in a whole new way. It creates "out of the box" thinking of how you perceive and approach the client and what he/she wants out of your product or service because the necessary focus is not on you, your company or your product but rather it is what the client wants to have or achieve. The companies that are directly responsible for making this happen get rewarded greatly. This is an incredibly liberating line of thinking because you and your company are no longer bound by the "laws" of product centric thinking. You are not having a square peg that you are judiciously trying to fit into a customer's round hole. What you are doing is to find out about the shape and dimensions of what the customer's round hole is and then you are shaping your product to fit into their use values.

Consider some of the companies that are listed. They think of their products as enhancing your life and not necessarily on the physical attributes of the product or the conventional industry thinking of the products or the customer. This does two things simultaneously:

1. Creates "out-of-the-box" thinking – hence, cars that park themselves (Lexus LS460), bookstores that allow you to read a whole book if you want (Barnes and Noble), beds and pillows that are designed to give a good night's sleep (Sheraton's Heavenly Bed), reinventing the coffee shop into a social scene or alternative workstation (Starbuck's), etc.

2. Removes or distances price-bound thinking because you, as the consumer, start to see the uniqueness of the company and its product from beyond just cars, hotel rooms, etc. The more the product/company becomes more unique in the mind of the consumer, the more it becomes a brand, that is, different from the rest of the market sellers. And that diminishes the effect that pricing has on the buying equation. How else can you explain the reason why Louis Vuitton purses and bags can sell at

such a premium when you can just as easily go out and purchase a no-name hand purse at a fraction of the cost?

If these companies can achieve these results by thinking of the business process, then why can't it be applied to your situation and with your product? The natural rebuttal would be that you don't have a huge R&D budget along with a market research firm to help you create this paradigm shift. Add to that the fact that you are not the CEO of the firm to create this quantum shift change for your firm.

However, you truly do not need any of that to change the operative thinking and approach by which to engage your current and potential clients. Of course, it helps if you are of the CEO or C band level but it is not mandatory. The key is to think of what it is that the client truly values beyond the obvious features.

CASE CITING – How Barnes & Noble won

In 1971, a young man named Leonard Riggio was working part-time at the bookstore for the college he was attending when he decided to leave university. He left because he knew he could do a much better job running a bookstore than his current boss did – and he didn't need a college degree to do it. Riggio's vision of a complete bookstore was very different from the traditional bookstore of the time. He was tired of stuffy, confined stores where the "average Joe" would feel uncomfortable searching for their latest literary fix.

So Riggio created an unprecedented literary empire – one with comfy chairs and tables where patrons could sit and read (even books not yet purchased), with public restrooms and an open environment. Throughout his tenure as CEO of the company Barnes & Noble (you may have heard of it), he has broken down barriers that were once dictated as fundamental to the book-selling community. His stores stock books covering an enormous range of subjects, serving an unbelievable range of clients.

His innovation didn't stay confined to the traditional selling space. When Amazon.com staked its claim as "the world's largest bookstore", Riggio wasn't about to be outdone. BarnesandNoble.com currently produces a satisfying 10% of all the company's profits – a strong answer to the growing need for businesses to function virtually as well as physically.

---

cont'd

Riggio's favorite example of why Barnes & Noble works as well as it does is the Barnes & Noble situated in urban Manhattan. There, you can find suited professionals sipping latte in the bookstore café alongside a homeless woman, copying passages from the biography of a surrealist poet. Why here instead of the library? Because, she answers, the lighting and air is so much better than the library, and there is pleasant music playing. [14] [15] [16]

Personal Case Citing –
From Zero to Hero by Re-thinking the "Problem"

Starting out in the mortgage industry, I was tasked as a wholesale mortgage banker to sell my firm's mortgage financing at a rate of 10.25%. The mortgage rate market was at 10%. My customers laughed me out of their offices.

As you may well know, a difference of .25% was huge compared to those people who were locking in their interest rates at 10% or 9.75%, which my customers (the mortgage brokers) got through other mortgage banks.

Panic set in! How can one sell money (the most homogenous and intangible thing in the world) and be able to differentiate the product to the degree that you can override the difference of .25%?

Desperation, and not necessity, is the mother of invention. I started to realize that there were other factors that played into the "buying" equation; factors such as:

- Underwriting turnaround time. Due to the demand for lower rates, the other banks were overwhelmed and their underwriting of the loan (loan approval) times were hovering around 30 days. My underwriting time was around 5 days.

- Lock in times for interest rates. Most banks had 15 day lock-ins (worthless especially in light of the 30 days underwriting times) but mine was 30 days which encompassed the time it took to close.

- Underwriting stringency. Other banks with the low rates were extremely strict and unforgiving of any credit "blemishes". My underwriters were able to balance out with mitigating factors such as job stability and good reserves.

As I began to approach my desperate customers (the mortgage brokers) on why it would be to their benefit to close loans faster and more readily with us than with the banks that had the lower rates of interest, business was starting to flow my way. So much business came to me (at a 25 basis point premium on the interest rate) that I finished out the year as member of the President's Club (top producers) of my company's network. I won that distinction for two consecutive years.

The aforementioned case citing is illustrative of how seemingly insurmountable differences are actually not so daunting when you see beyond the attributes (physical or otherwise) of your product or service. It also serves to point out that even my very astute customers didn't "see" the underlying advantages of what I had to offer until it was highlighted to them. Sometimes, even the customer isn't aware of what they really need until it is brought to light.

Proposition: How you see the product is the product. Your perception will help to determine how the client perceives your use value to him/her.

If you see what you offer as a series of features and attributes (usually physical aspects that are commonly accepted) by which you seek to satisfy your customer's needs, you will have cheated yourself and your client of a very large part of what may establish you and your product as unique, distinct, and special to a client.

Remember, the second byproduct of concentrating on what the customer would like to derive from your product: a certain elasticity in terms of pricing in purchasing decisions. What else can justify why the aforementioned brands demand a price premium above their peers?

Question: What other product is more homogenous and non-distinguishable than money? Consider this, the only differentiation of one bank's money from another bank is the cost of it (in the form of the interest rate and "points") and the terms of it — that's essentially it! But in the personal case citing of my experience in the mortgage market, it really wasn't just about the cost of money, was it?

There was a multiplicity of factors that helped to establish a difference that my clients (the mortgage brokers) could see and then in turn sell to their clients (the home buyers). But, at first, the mortgage brokers could not see "value" in being .25% more expensive because that is the gauge that they were applying to every opportunity that came across their desk. And for a time I got sucked into that product-centric thinking. However, having thought through the process and seeing the opportunities from the overloaded mortgage market, I was able to highlight that which was truly important to mortgage brokers and the home buyers – a closed loan!! In the example given, the closed and funded loan is the true use value to the home buyer, home seller, and agents involved because, by the successful completion of that process, is what causes everyone to achieve their goals.

In uncovering and targeting what the customer derives from your product beyond that which is surface- or product-centric in nature, you are liberated to think on levels that will challenge how you and others look at the use value of your product. In thinking in these unorthodox terms, you are then free to innovate and tailor the message to highlight how your product may truly fulfill your customer's true uses and perceptions in unique ways. Those unique ways is what establishes you and your product as a "brand". Personal branding will be covered very extensively later in this book which will show how you can create your own personal brand and have a branding experience with your clients.

You, your company, and even your client (with your help) will learn to think along different and more productive lines if you reconsider what it is that the client really wants versus what it is that you really have to offer to him/her. But, in order to do so, you need to shed old/ineffective thinking and re-think your world view. How you do that is to go back and look at the very powerful effects that bad patterns have on our lives.

Chapter 6:
Know Thyself:
Ridding Yourself of Bad Patterns

Identify Bad Patterns

You truly need to see current patterns of conduct that exist in you, your company, and the client which have either helped or hampered growth and development. These patterns need to be re-assessed in order to be modified, eliminated, or promoted. Let's talk about the bad patterns.

The "Spiral of Terror"

As a result of pressures to make sales no matter what the cost in today's complex business environment, many professionals find themselves caught in a downward spiral. This "Spiral of Terror" proceeds through the following cycle:

Pressure of Quotas → Desperation → Push to Make the Sale → Results in Poor Decisions

Think about it. Do sellers that are NOT desperate make "stupid" moves or decisions? Most likely not. Why? Because they measure twice and cut once in their dealings and they have a sense of control which is communicated to the buyer that they will not sell at any price or terms just to seal the deal. So what happens when you feel that you have a gun to your head? The natural human tendency is to react in an anxious and fear-filled manner. This then produces the following actions:

1. **Tunnel Vision**: Focusing too much on getting the client to "close" or finalize the transaction becomes the main purpose and as a result it blinds the seller to the other ways to approach clients other than using the crude and readily obvious tools such as features, terms, and pricing. This self-inflicted myopia severely reduces the ability of the seller in working with the buyer on an equal footing, thus crippling the seller's chances of negotiating to their own advantage.

2. **Dispersion:** This could be one of two things:

   a. Trying to throw features or benefits at clients to see what "sticks". This is a method by which the seller uses rapid fire approach of "peppering" the client with features and benefits of the product to determine which of them has traction with the client. This is a very primitive method because inherent in adoption of this approach is the idea that the seller has done little or no homework on the buyer or the situation.

   b. Feature-throwing is only as effective as the client who is driven by the one dimensional aspects of product-driven thinking. That one product driven need once met by various sellers then leads to the next differentiator which is pricing. Pricing is the Achilles heel of this approach because, unless you hurdle it (which invariably means lowering the price), then you will only be perceived as running with the pack. No better, no worse. Yuck!

   c. Going after as many projects, assignments, and clients as much as possible. The operative thinking is that, with the amount of exposure to all these people and events, the possibility of success is increased. However, what is not considered is the fact that the relationships and knowledge that comes from this dispersion technique is usually shallow and not long term.

   d. The blind RFPs, the blind auctions, and the shotgun approach to marketing all carry an equalizing effect upon what you are trying to achieve -- which is exactly the opposite of what you should want. You should want to differentiate yourself from the rest of the market in a very strong and positive fashion. Not to be equalized with the competition.

3. **"Speed Dating":** This is the kissin' cousin of Dispersion. The premise is much like the social phenomenon of "speed dating" wherein strangers are forced to, in a matter of minutes, interact through question/answer, statements, and anecdotes to ascertain if there is enough potential for the other person to be a possible mate. The business version of this

phenomenon is meeting with as many clients and in a brief moment of time determine whether there is potential to do business. The result is that attrition (the systematic tossing out relationships that don't work *immediately)* of "weak" clients occurs in favor of more appealing or possibly more rewarding clients. There may be some defensible position to this approach but I can't seem to find any. The problem with this is that what you may think as "weak" clients (think: local or regional players) may actually have business needs and resources than more appealing (think: big market dominant leaders) companies.

What I've found to be true is that global companies, due to their size, are usually very:

a. Cumbersome to work with (not only does the left hand not know what the right hand is doing; sometimes they don't even know that the right hand even exists).

b. Bureaucratic. Having to go through so many layers of approval that any decision is akin to elephantine gestation periods.

c. Arrogant. Because they are the biggest, then the mindset is that they are the "baddest" on the block and there needs be special concessions to them regardless of circumstances.

d. Impotent. Yes, I meant that statement. The largest companies are not usually market leaders in exploring new ways of doing things and taking calculated risks that smaller firms are known for (usually due to necessity). As a result, there usually is a very arduous process in which to enact anything new or working with new vending partners. This tendency neutralizes a lot of actions and initiatives that may be started with smaller (perceived as "weaker") firms.

4. **Undue Pressure**: This comes from intensifying the process of client engagements by applying ever- increasing levels of pressure to close the "deal". The goal is to effect faster client decision-making and execution by using various techniques (e.g., constant badgering, new product line introductions or promotions) to put up the "numbers". It makes the mistake of equating the speed in which you get closed purchase

transactions as an acceptable form of selling. What really comes from this approach is a lot of problems in making and closing transactions that are not to the seller's advantage. While this may be perceived as how to do business, really what you have done as the selling company is to create an environment of self-inflicted pressure and artificial timelines that water down your brand. Just as injurious to your efforts is the perception by clients that you are being a "pest" or that you are "desperate".

5. **Quota Driven Thinking**: Whoa!! Did I just write that in there? Yes, I did, being fully cognizant of the near-heretical stance that the statement makes. Don't misunderstand; quotas are necessary and when properly used and managed, they give clarity to purpose. However, what I am referring to is the quota driven <u>thinking</u> much like the aforementioned types of "Spiral of Terror" variations, quota-driven thinking puts too much emphasis on transactions and the tangible end-results. While in the short run this thinking tends to be effective due to the intensity that it evokes, however, for longevity purposes this type of paradigm is woefully detrimental to further business and growth into other areas as its main emphasis is invariably the "here and now". Quotas are very necessary benchmarks by which to judge the performance of your sales team and that is undisputed. The problem comes in how to use quotas. In very few organizations are potential clients viewed in tiered timelines or levels of engagement. All clients are not alike and the bigger they are, the more the timelines need to be stretched out as behemoths seldom turn on a dime in getting projects up and running. The unnatural application of time pressures tends to create the next and final bad pattern.

6. **Making the sale at all costs**: The worst thing anyone or any organization can do is to make a sale at any cost. People are like animals and they will sense your need to sell your product or service even at disadvantageous levels or terms. Why? Because most people are poor poker players and give signals of their desperation without consciously meaning to do so. Here are some key signs of desperation:

Acceptance of "unacceptable" terms. Would you accept "unlimited liability" in contract negotiations? Would you be alright with one-sided termination or severability clauses in contract? Does your firm allow punitive damages for non-performance or not living up to certain service level agreements (SLAs)? Are payment terms of net 90 days or 120 days or even 180 days acceptable? If the answer is yes, then guess what? You are telegraphing your need to close the transaction as a weak partner. This may be de rigeur when working for monolithic, global entities, but I have been party to many transactions with these giants and had them re-work or reconfigure based on what was equitable and not what they solely wanted.

Badgering or compression selling. This means to close the selling transaction by virtually peppering the client to close via email, phone or multiple meetings. It means not being able to keep within the lines of proper sales tenacity and crossing over to annoyance or irritation. This does nothing but diminish your credibility with the potential client. The thought that comes to mind is "why are they so desperate to make this happen"? Is there a problem with liquidity? With reputation? With product? Truthfully, wouldn't you question someone's motives if they were hell bent to close the deal such as in purchasing a car? Is this a lemon that they are trying to unload?

Pricing that is not at par with market pricing. This is a key indicator of desperation. Would you buy a Mercedes at the price of a Kia? And, if so, then why would it be sold at that level? When buyers catch wind of this then what happens is a "limbo stick" effect on how low you can get the seller to go before it becomes a no-go situation.

I have personally seen companies sell at a really low level just to get the business and thereby bulking up their market share. This strategy has never worked for long-term relationships because it is predominantly driven by pricing and any temporary win of market share could be wiped out by a commensurate decrease in pricing by the competition or by the seller's costs going up to wipe out any profit there might be. Loss leaders, promotions, or discounting are nefarious for this kind of signaling of seller desperation. It's like going to battle, and even before the troops have engaged, you send out ambassadors to pound out an amicable truce.

No pushbacks. In the never-ending need to please the client, a lot of firms have said yes and agreed to some really egregious terms, conditions, pricing and positioning. When there are no legitimate pushbacks in terms of any of the above criteria, then buyers who aren't even bullies would see how far they can push the situation to their advantage. This is only natural and yet many selling firms don't see it.

There are many more bad practices -- too many to practically enumerate and describe -- but these stand out as common foibles. They epitomize the old school of selling. They tend to look at people as units and business relationships as transactions. These approaches, while effective on a very short-term basis, are nonetheless very ineffective over the long term because they treat clients/ customers as units, promote a shallow understanding of the clients due to the need for speed, and are very transactionally based in terms of client thinking.

Let's be very honest with ourselves. There are some clients that need to be fired. They are only your clients because you have caved into them time and time again. They are not even nice to you in the process. These are the same individuals and companies that will leave you in a heartbeat if there is a better (even marginally better) competing offer. Why do you want that? It is very tenuous ground to walk on and can only further cheapen your reputation with them and the marketplace overall.

To summarize, these bad, sad patterns feed upon each other and devolve into a state of freneticism and frantic behavior that does not promote lasting revenue production much less strong, resilient business relationships. The death of these behaviors cannot come too swiftly.

The next key point in "knowing thyself" comes from questioning old, accepted definitions that have held us back. Follow this train of thought:

IF: How we define things is how we look at things **THEN** how we look at things determines how we approach situations.

IF: How we approach situations determines the success or failure of ventures **THEN** it is very crucial (to close the loop) on how we define things!

One of the most powerful and yet improperly defined words on the planet is "value". And from this misinterpreted word comes a lot of problems in selling and the interaction between seller and buyer as we shall see next.

Chapter 7:
The Misunderstandings Over "Value"

Pretend, for a moment, that you are a doctor and that you have before you a body to examine so you can find out what the problems are. But this body isn't a human one. Rather, it is a corporate "body". The corporate body is a firm that sells its products and services in the marketplace. The patient is complaining of various pains: some sharp and sudden, while others are a dull, aching pain. As a good doctor, you would try to map out as many of these complaints as possible to achieve a "holistic" view of the body and its dysfunctions. After an extensive interview, you find out that these are the conditions that exist right now:

Classic Model	Current Model
Contracts are written for multi-year timeframes	Contracts are written for one year or less, with substantial termination clauses
Contracts are made by key personnel or departments	Contracts have a multi-party approval process
Procurement performed internally	Procurement performed by outsourced entities
Companies rely on one or two vending partners for multiple year timeframes	Companies source out to many vendors for short stints
Bidding for business is based on value, price, performance, and stability	Reverse auction bidding is used, heavily weighted upon the "lowest bidder" mentality
Contracts allow increases based on cost of inflation, etc.	Contracts have built-in price reductions required of the vendor on a year-by-year basis, ignoring inflationary realities
Cost of doing business is shared between the buyer and the seller	Cost of doing business (such as inventory, transportation, etc.) are pushed to the seller (vendors)
More parity exists in the relationship between the buyer and the seller	Due to the aggregate market power of certain key buyers, there exists very lopsided power relationships between buyer and seller

Now that we know what the patient is complaining about (symptoms) and the conditions and lifestyle habits of the patient (operative thinking), then what is left is to draw from these facts as to the root source of the ailments (the disease).

Generally speaking, the problem all stems from the degradation of the seller's position in the markets. In working with buyers, the sellers have given a lot of ground just to enjoy the little piece of business that they currently have. This disturbing trend is exactly what is happening in the real world and, as a result, companies that sell products/services are feverishly trying to regain ground again! Different initiatives that I have seen are:

- Repackaging of products/services

- Re-pricing of products/services

- Promotions of short duration

- Bundling of products/services to create more "value"

- New features such as dashboards, diagnostic or feedback mechanisms to make their products more "sexy"

- Re-branding of the company or its products/services

There is a hand-wringing search for the "magic bullet" that will help to shore up the seller's position. And while some efforts do have a short-term effectiveness, nonetheless, the results are just stimulus packaging.

So what does work? What is left? What you begin to hear in the strategy meeting rooms of marketing, sales, and account management teams is this word called "value". More specifically, you will hear "value proposition" or "value statement" or some variant that involves "value" to counter these trends.

The operative thinking behind the "value"-driven client management approach is that if you can create "value" in the eyes of your client, then they will buy into your product or service more readily than if you didn't do so. This seems to be the correct way and from my experiences and those of many others, it has been a good route to follow. However, what is left is the question: what will you hinge "value" upon? Is it the product/service you offer? Is it an aspect of the product such as: price, utility, accuracy, quality, etc.? Let's look at two major schools of thought:

Value-From-Product Fallacy

Consider this: everyone in the marketplace is constantly looking for a <u>competitive advantage</u>. Whether it is in the features of the product, contractual terms and conditions, service delivery, pricing, partnering, or technological advances, everyone is looking for the "edge" over their competition. But, how long will that "edge" last once it is attained? Couldn't the competition evolve to match and overtake whatever edge your company can muster? The answer is – they certainly can and will.

Case Citing – What happens when cutting edge becomes boring

Lest you think that your industry or product line's technological competitive advantages are impervious to the effects of being overtaken or mitigated by the marketplace, then consider the following:

In 2009, I made a call to my Swedish friend Fredrik who is visiting me where I am located in New Jersey. My call, originating in New Jersey, goes from my phone to the nearest cell tower and out to switches and routers that push the call out to the Stockholm area. In Sweden, Fredrik's phone company's router then sends the call signal back out to the US.

The call then is routed to Fredrik's phone located somewhere in New Jersey (which, knowing Fredrik, is either at a first-rate department store or a pub). There is, of course, tons of technical detail that was glossed over in this short description. However, all this switching back and forth of a call signal between the locations of New Jersey area to Stockholm area (3910 miles or 6292 kilometers – just one way) takes a matter of seconds! Yet, we don't even think about it.

This act would've been considered prohibitively expensive 20 years ago and science fiction about 40 years ago, especially considering the speed and ease by which it is done. Yet, what was once thought of as Buck Rogers-type of technology has become commonplace. So much so that when we place a call to Russia, we don't even think of the seismic changes in technology, politics and lifestyles that had to occur for such a product offering to even be conceived of much less executed.

A further illustration of the product fallacy:

Case Citing – Whiz Bang!

Cell Phones

When Motorola first came out with the DynaTac 8000X (the brick-sized forerunner to the modern cell phone), it was priced at $4,000 in 1983 and the cost of a minute back then was 50 cents per minute with a $6 per month user fee. A one-hour conversation would cost $30!! The DynaTac 8000X was also severely limited in terms of functionalities and range.

Compare that with the current costs: some phones can be purchased for as low as $70, with a rate of only .7 cents per minute (less than a penny) depending upon the contract signed.[17]

Microwaves

In 1947, Raytheon demonstrated the world's first microwave oven and called it a "Radarange," the winning name in an employee contest. Housed in refrigerator-sized cabinets, the first microwave ovens cost between $2,000 and $3,000. Between 1952 and 1955, Tappan introduced the first home model priced at $1,295. In 1965, Raytheon acquired Amana Refrigeration. Two years later, the first countertop, domestic oven was introduced. It was a 100-volt microwave oven, which cost just under $500 and was smaller, safer and more reliable than previous models. [18]

The price of these products have dropped precipitously from what they used to be and the rate of innovation and obsolescence is only increasing with technology gains, thereby reducing any "competitive advantage" time that one may enjoy. The aforementioned companies were leaders in their respective industries and known for leading edge technological breakthroughs – they were the "Apple" of their day. Now, these companies have seen that their killer applications become as mundane and generic as cereal in the morning.

So it begs the question: if your product, specifications, features, benefits, capabilities, etc. are not enough to give you a sustainable competitive advantage, then what is left? Adding more bells and whistles?

Bundling or solutions selling is predicated on the idea that having a bundling of features and characteristics will help to build more value in the product or service rendered. While that may, on a logical basis, be a reasonable statement to make, there is one troubling reality. What if you did bundling of products/services but the client still didn't want to buy it or buy it at the price at which you are trying to sell it? Having been on the selling side of too many proposals and product presentations, I have not seen a direct correlation in results that would support the statement that, if you bulked up a product with more attributes or other ancillary features, then you get more interest from the buyer to either buy or buy at the asked-for price.

This frustrates the living daylights out of the sellers! They rant and rave that the buyer is either mentally deficient or too greedy in asking for a lower price for more product. And all the while the point is missed. Maybe, just maybe, the buyer really wasn't that impressed with the add-ons to begin with.

If I am not perceiving any worth in the original price of something as a standalone item, then why would I be more interested to purchase the product just because other things were bolted onto it? If the seller has not uncovered my real uses for the product in question (and in doing so find out how important the product is in my world), then bundling or solutions selling isn't going to motivate me to buy the product any more than if it stood alone.

An example of the preceding bundling conundrum: Dashboards and diagnostic/visibility tools are heavily relied upon by consultancies to justify to the client the added value of what they are trying to purvey. And while these attributes may be of value to clients, a lot of consultancies and businesses default to the idea that these dashboards will be the clincher in getting the client to perceive that real value has been attained due to this unprecedented visibility offered. I can't tell you how many clients have NOT purchased systems due to these value adds. In the end, the purchase was made regardless but the dashboards were a "nice to haves" and not "must haves".

Value-From-Price Fallacy

One of the worst culprits of "classic" client or sales thinking pertains to pricing (or more accurately the role that price plays in transactions). Pricing seems to a lot of people like an immutable law of physics. "What goes up must come down" and the like. If your price is higher than others (in an RFP situation or not), then your chances of winning the bid are slim to none. Correct?

And yet, there are companies that offer their products/services at higher prices than others and it is accepted by very astute buying firms. But we all know that there are companies offering products at lower prices and whose functionality may be at the same level as these higher end companies but they don't get selected. Does that make sense in a perfectly rational market? No? I didn't think so. If you apply logic to pricing, then it is anything but immutable. Let's take a look at what role pricing plays in the RFP process.

The Modern RFP and Price

The premise of the modern RFP (request for proposal) is to create a fairly level playing field with which to observe, measure, and judge vendors on pre-set criteria. Apart from the performance attributes of the product or service which would be specific to the transaction, some of the common pre-set criteria are:

- *Timeframes*

- *Guarantees*

- *Service levels*

- *Terms and conditions*

- *Financial strength of your company (or lack thereof)*

This list is just a short sample. But I have purposely left out the one major sieve that most people use to measure others – Price.

Price has been the altar upon which many sellers or bidders have sacrificed their profits to satiate the need for acceptance by the buyer. While some buyers, putting their business out to bid, have taken to saying that price is not the "only deciding factor", the fact remains that it is a heavily weighted factor as compared to the rest.

But assuming that your product is not outrageously priced as compared to what the market is offering, what then is the reason for price reductions to clinch the transaction or at least the operative thinking behind such a move? The question is asked: would a greater value be derived from your product from the buyer (user) as a result of dropping the rates? I think anyone who says "yes" to the previous statement would be hard pressed to cling to that answer if they were to think about the question in terms of "(use) value derived from your product"

Reality Check – Is value contingent on price?

People use the word value in a free form way, such as, "That purchase was a great value!" or "I bought two at that price, man, what a value!" But are they talking about "value" or are they talking about "price"?

Let's be specific: Say you go to a store that offers two toothpaste tubes for the price of one. The normal statement would be "what a great value!" However, the value of the toothpaste to you (to help fight cavities, freshen your breath, or whiten your teeth) -- has that increased? Is the use you derive enhanced by the price? Did the lower price make your mouth twice as minty or your teeth twice as bright? No. What you got was more product for the same price you would have purchased for one tube.

Well then, why were you talking about "value"? Or were you talking about the great deal on toothpaste you got from the 2-for-1 pricing? I think most people mistake the statement of lower price with greater "value" and this is a great example of the mixing of metaphors.

Why is it important to make a distinction between "value" and "price"? Because the common perception that people work from is that the lower the "price" of a product then the more "value" you derive from a product. People and corporate buying or procurement departments think along those lines. You, as a seller, may think that way as well. But that simply isn't true. And how you think and approach that issue makes a big difference as to how you will successfully beat the price dependent thinking.

As sellers, we tend to think in this fashion as it pertains to value:

1. The more features and bundling I offer with my product or service at the same or lower price than the competition, then the more value I am giving the buyer.

2. The more product quantities that I give at the same or lower price than the competition, then the more value I am giving the buyer.

But is value related to price? Or is a buyer's valuation of a product or service hinged on something totally different? The understanding of value versus price relationship is crucial in the breaking of bad thinking that has kept many people chained to pricing as a yardstick for measuring value.

Value as it Relates to Price

Let's consider the following train of thought on value and pricing:

1. People buy things for the use that they derive out of it. Those can be real and tangible such as can openers in opening up food cans so that you can prepare a meal. Or those uses can be intangible such as the enjoyment or aesthetic pleasure that one derives from a diamond ring.

(So far, so good?)

2. Pricing comes in to try and determine a "value" to the use that is derived from items and objects based upon what the market will pay for it – the level of pricing usually dependent on the scarcity or intrinsic cost of the item. Diamonds are scarcer than can openers so they are radically more expensive.

(Still with me?)

3. However, the word "value" muddies things up because we try to equate the pricing of a thing to the "value" of that thing. There are two examples of this:

a. Proposition: The more expensive the item, the more value we derive/enjoy from that item (e.g., diamonds, sports cars).

b. Proposition: Or in another way of defining "value", the more of that object we acquire with lower price, then the more we have gotten "value" or worth out of that transaction (i.e., 2-for-1 sales).

But these two "value" statements are not necessarily accurate or true. See below.

4. Consider the examples of a can opener and a very expensive diamond ring. Most normal thinking would say that the can opener has little value compared to a diamond ring and so the price is reflective of that fact. However, if you were out in the wilderness during a severe snowstorm stuck in a log cabin for weeks (wearing your diamond ring) with a very large supply shelf full of canned foods but no can opener in sight, then what happens to the "value" of things? It becomes radically different, doesn't it? Unless you found an alternative way to open up those cans, you probably would exchange your very expensive diamond ring for one rusted but useable can opener. So the value of something (i.e., the can opener) shot up dramatically due to the fact that its <u>use</u> far exceeded that of the diamond ring because, if you didn't have it, then you would probably starve.

An extreme example, yes, but one that, in its extremity, illustrates the concept of <u>use value</u> in determining what is or is not of "value".

5. So the "value" of something at any given moment in time (and the values change quickly sometimes) comes from the "use" or "use value" that you get from a product and not from the market price of that product, right? If in doubt, then the quote from Richard III by Shakespeare may help. When surrounded at the battle of Bosworth Field, King Richard III was desperate to escape with his life but had no horse to do so. King Richard III, assessing the situation, uttered the immortal phrase, "A horse! A horse! My kingdom for a horse!" So the use value of a horse suddenly became equal to that of a kingdom because that is what King Richard saw as a means by which to extricate himself from danger. NOTE: It was to no avail because he died at that battle.

6. The scarcity of a product or the intrinsic cost of a product (e.g., flat panel HD television sets) may have an effect on price but it is the use value that one derives from the product that really sets the price. NOTE: the use value may be of a tangible real nature (like the can opener) or intangible and subjective (like the diamond ring).

7. Another example can be given in a very expensive bottle of wine. If I have no taste for wine and actually don't drink any alcohol at all, then I have no use value for the product except as a re-gifting present or to sell on an online wine auction. So no matter how low the price may be lowered (or even given for free), if I do not perceive any use value from the wine, then I would not be interested in acquiring such a bottle no matter what the price may be. There is no use value in the actual product and its manifold attributes (taste, smell, looks, etc.) and so there is no transaction, regardless of the market price.

What, then, is Value related to?

Value, as we have seen in the two previous sections, is not based on product (features, characteristics, specifications) or price. Value seems to be an amorphous or very poorly defined thing and there is reason for this lack of concrete definition as it pertains to value. Value is murky to spell out because it is in the eye of the beholder. You can have 500 people in a room looking over a car or boat or anything and you will get 500 valuations on the worth of that object in question. The value of a car could range from zero to thousands of dollars depending on the car and the person that is judging the valuation of the car. Why? Because some people have no use for cars due to lifestyle and others may covet a certain type of car (collector, muscle cars, antique) and would gladly pay top dollar for one.

With such a universally splintered way of looking at something, then how can any person (or company), no matter how big or knowledgeable, be able to come up with a valid "value proposition" or "value statement"? It is nearly impossible to cookie cut the value of a product or service so that you can, with pinpoint accuracy, say that this product or service with these features and with this price is the true value of something EVEN IF THERE IS A MARKET PRICE that is established for the product or service.

Yes, even if you say that something is worth $100 (such as a gun), the valuation of it (in terms of buyers) is still dependent on what that specific, individual buyer may judge as its worth. For someone who abhors guns and the idea or thought of owning or using such a thing, then the value would be zero. For someone seeking protection from such a product, then it would be worth $100. If the gun was one that finished a collection, then they may pay double or more to acquire it.

So, borrowing from the example just given, if you were a gun seller, then you had better find out the attitude or disposition of the potential customer to whom you are approaching to sell pistols. And therein lies the answer to selling based on value. The value of something is based on the beholder's (buyer's) view and so, if you uncover their perception of use (no use = no value, great use = great value), then you will have gotten a very good handle on whether there will be a sale and at approximately what price.

I know this sounds very basic -- almost elementary -- but a lot of professional people get hung up on this principle of value. They look at the product or service rendered and try to extract value hooks from features/benefits so that they can present this to the customer and see if they agree rather than listening to the customer and learning what their expectation of what the product's uses should be.

The next Personal Case Citing illustrates the idea of uncovering a customer's uses in order to win them over and it happened to my brother.

Personal Case Citing – How to love a used car salesman

Sometime ago, my older brother, Paul, found himself between jobs in his storied career as a hotelier. He was working as a bartender when someone approached him to contemplate being a car salesman for a Hyundai dealer. Paul took up the offer and then asked his kid brother (me) what my approach was to winning over customers.

I winced when I heard that he had done so especially without consulting with me prior to such a "rash" move! I told him that he was biting off quite a lot because, in my decades-long career in sales, I had never contemplated working in such a harsh environment.

The customers really have a very bad mindset about the people and transaction prior to going to an auto dealer and that it was akin to going into a boxing ring everyday with different opponents.

Nevertheless, Paul pressed on and asked me what I think would help in terms of changing that hostile environment to one that was more conducive to sales. I said that, even though I knew nothing about car sales, I did know a thing or two about selling in negative environments.

I said that, in a negative selling setup, the key was to allay the clients concerns and co-opt him in the process of making the sale. In other words, work with the customer to come to a decision as to whether they want to buy the car or not and, if so, then at what price point and features. The consultative model of sales is extremely powerful in getting rid of the animosity of distrustful buyers. Paul took to heart what I said but what he did next was nothing short of AMAZING!!

A few months passed and I called him to find out what was going on with his new endeavor, and he stated that it went well (very well, indeed)! Paul created a sheet of paper that could be used on a clipboard. The sheet of paper would have the following type of information.

Characteristics	Paul's Hyundai Dealer	Dealer X	Dealer Y
What do you currently drive?			
What type of car are you looking at?			
What do you mainly use the car for?			
Who will be the principal driver of the car? Where do you drive to/from most of the time?			
When do you typically drive? Weekday? Weekend?			
What do you use the vehicle for? Kids transport? Home business?			

Based on the answers, given Paul would then recommend a car befitting the situation, then talk about the price with options, and finally discuss the financing plan that would spell out how much down payment was needed for the kind of payment that they could afford. Then, as a kicker, Paul would give them the sheet to take to another dealer down the street to have an across-the-board comparison before he would sell them anything. Paul said to the customers, as they were leaving, that if his analysis and pricing was better, then he would be more than happy to sell the car to them upon their return, which was an audacious move in any sales person's world!

This stunned the potential customers. They couldn't believe that they weren't harassed and barraged with opening/closing techniques in trying to push them to a consummation of the sale right there and then. Some of them didn't quite know what to do as they were walking away from this very odd car salesman that refused for them to buy the car from that one visit.

The customers came back! At least 88% of them (Paul tracked them) and made him #1 or #2 top salesperson of that dealership from his second month to his last month (18 months later). In addition, Paul consistently got repeat business and referrals from his growing cadre of happy customers! He was the envy of the dealership's crew of salespeople. By the way, there were approximately 20+ salespeople that he consistently beat who were die hard veterans at the "game".

Postscript: Note how Paul's approach was all about the customer and more importantly what their uses were as it related to the car they were contemplating purchasing. Some of the customers even changed their mind (thinking they were going to buy model X and ending up buying model Y) because the use chart had led them to a different but superior decision. Notice also that Paul really didn't have to "sell"; he just helped to uncover the customer's uses for the vehicle and the buyers came to the conclusion that the Hyundais were the best deal pound for pound. The fact that they liked Paul's style didn't hurt.

Value is so unique that to do anything other than find out what the client really wants out of your product, your company, or you is really condemning yourself to a lot of frustration in trying to GUESS the answer when it can be TOLD to you.

Use Value is Key

So what does this all mean? It means that value does not equal price but rather use value equals price. Use value is the usage of a product or service and its valuation can go up or down very quickly dependent on the situation or the market or both.

PROPOSITIONS:

A. The true value of something is in the USE the client can gain from that something (product, service, or company that provides either). In other words, use of something determines its worth (value) to the buyer or user and NOT the price of the product. Another way of saying this is: buyers (clients) have use values for the products that are in the marketplace. The higher the use values of a product, the more the client is willing to pay to attain it.

B. It is imperative to know your client's use value (or usages) of your product, company or of you. In order to be successful, you need to know what their motivation for purchasing is and at what price it would be.

Stated plainly:
VALUE does not equal PRICE
VALUE is not related to PRICE
VALUE is equal to the USE of something
USE VALUE = the worth of the uses (hidden or otherwise) of something in the eye of the beholder
USE VALUE dictates PRICE (that a buyer is willing to pay)

If use value is not enhanced either by the lowering or the increasing of price, then why is price used (by both seller and buyer) as a major determinant for success in a transaction? Why is the measure of a purchasing transaction so tied to the ultimate price of a product? Here are some reasons:

✓ Price is easy to quantify, measure, and compare

✓ Price shows the purchase transaction results readily

Most people use price as a point of negotiation because it is the simplest criterion with which to work. Notice I did not mention affordability in the context of price negotiations.

REALITY CHECK –
Corporate Budgets are not Personal Budgets

Price is usually held up as a very large factor for decision-making, especially when an RFP (request for proposal) is involved. When a company states that they are keeping to a budget to make it affordable for themselves, there is something subliminal that happens to a selling/vending party. I believe that most selling people equate this to the dynamic of what happens in their own personal finances.

Don't mix up your views on affordability with companies' version of affordability. With personal affordability, it is generally based on rationing of scarce resources. Hence most people cannot buy a Porsche but instead opt for a Volkswagen.

This subliminal effect is that the selling side takes it as a "given" that they must lower the price to conform to usually an undefined "budget" threshold.

Companies also have limited resources; however, their limits are vastly bigger than private individuals'. And they have alternative sources of financing not even offered to individuals. It has been my experience that if a company wants to "budget" for a project, then it gets done. Budget is code word for allocation. Allocation is driven by prioritization. Prioritization is structured by perception.

The Problem with Price

No one would ever begrudge a buyer who wants to pay the "best" price for the product that they want. Price, however, is all too often used by buyers as a tool to promote their own agenda. Whether the agenda is one of exclusion, such as is the case of the buyer who has a hidden agenda that doesn't include you, or one in which the buyer treats everyone as a vendor and does their best to have the lowest possible rate always, this is often at the expense of the seller.

The odd thing about price is its almost universal acceptance as <u>the</u> primary measure for negotiation. This point is so unquestioned and accepted by both buyer and seller that to question its validity as a proper benchmark of transactional success seems almost heretical. The irony is that most sellers have also come to accept price as the operative and prime deciding factor in their talks with the buyer, <u>thus ensuring themselves of a price reduction</u>. Price has become the standard by which buyer and seller judge themselves as to whether they negotiated well or not. But do you see something wrong with this picture?

The problem with price is twofold in nature:

The first is that the business relationship based on price as the major component that binds them together is tenuous at very best. It is as good as the next price decrease (by the competitor) or increase (by the seller) for the product in question.

The second is even more fundamental. A business relationship that is predicated on a pseudo-adversarial relationship in which "my loss is your gain" really is not a very good platform for long term, sustainable growth and development (especially when based on something as fragile as pricing.) It is, however, great for transient, volatile, and highly charged interactions. If that is what you want, then that is what you will get.

Price also has a critical weakness. Price's one dimensionality precludes discussion on what really matters in business, which is the multiplicity of factors that goes into performing well together. The use values aren't addressed when you look at price, whether it is the seller or the buyer that concentrates on it.

Proposition: In the absence of a strong use value established in the mind of the client, then what will be emphasized are externals such as price, product attributes, etc.

This price fixation skews the thinking of how to look at real transactions with real consequences.

Personal Case Citing – When I mistook pricing for "value"

When I was as an account manager in the container ship industry, I was calling on a potential client (Company A) who was a very big shipper of computer peripherals from their US facilities to their customers in Europe and Asia.

My company had no share of their business and I wanted to find out why. In the first brief meeting, it was made very clear to me by the logistics and operations manager, Ms. Jones, that the reason why we didn't have any piece of their business was because of a very bad error in the past that we committed.

Three years prior, we had moved a 40-foot container of computer peripherals from West to East Coast by rail with the intent to catch one of our ships out from Montreal to Europe. Due to a sudden snowstorm, the container (along with thousands of other containers) was stuck in a rail facility for what turned out to be two additional weeks. The situation was exacerbated by the fact that we lost track of the container's true whereabouts due to the moving of a massive amount of containers to accommodate snow removal.

As a result, company A had to re-tool and re-make the model type and specifications of their product and then air ship the whole lot to their customer due to service level agreement requirements. This had cost their company $65,000 in costs. From that day forward, our company lost their business and Ms. Jones said (with pride) that she was my company's "sworn enemy".

Well, that was a wonderful meeting! But undaunted, I persisted in the next six months and Ms. Jones stated, offhandedly, that an RFP was soon to be issued requesting price quote and logistics proposal for containers coming out of one of their maquiladoras (factories on the Mexican side of the Mexico/US border) going to their customers in Europe. Ms. Jones said that I could participate in the RFP but she flatly stated that she doubted that we would be able to win. Why? Because of her abiding hatred of our company and the fact that the other competitors were the #1 and #3 largest and most powerful container lines in the world (at that time).

Challenged, I took the initiative to work hard on all the complexities of shipping containers out of a Mexican border town; complexities such as logistics planning, border issues, legality issues, risk issues – just to name a few. In an incredibly short amount of time, my team was able to punch through and address all these issues. One sticky point remained. That was price.

The price was too high, our landed costs were pinched, squeezed, and shaved as much as our operations people could extract out of such a complicated move that involved a lot of coordination.

There was simply no room to lower our costs anymore. The next thing that could be shaved was our profit margin. So, in my youth and inexperience, I worked hard to lower our margins by stating all the obvious "hot" buttons – "new client", "market share increase", "strategic partnering". Finally, the pricing manager said "Look man, we can't go any lower. To do so would make us underwater on these moves and I am not about to do that and neither should you!!"

I knew our pricing manager was right but I also knew that we were head and shoulders more expensive than what Ms. Jones would expect or that the competition would be. I knew we would not win this one, which was difficult to accept because I had worked so hard on this transaction.

It was a dark day when I turned our proposal into Ms. Jones. In less than a week, I got a phone call from Ms. Jones who gleefully told me that we lost the bid because, yes you guessed it, we were way too expensive! She told me that both #1 and #3 had won and that she knew that we were not going to win due to our poor company reputation. She definitely was rubbing salt into my wound.

It bothered me but I moved on to concentrate on better prospects. Irrationally, I was kind of mad at our pricing manager for not lowering the price. This loss proved to me the incontrovertible fact that pricing was key!

Then a strange thing occurred. A few weeks later, as I reviewed our booking sheets (these were logs of who was "booked" or reserved space on our vessels to ship with us), I saw that Company A had begun to book on my company's vessels. And before I could recover from the shock, I noticed that the bookings were for exactly the moves that I had lost on the RFP response!

I did something that I had never done before (or since). I didn't do a thing. I thought it a temporary aberration. I even thought it might have been a cruel joke by Ms. Jones. But as the following weeks rolled on, the bookings went from 1-2 containers a week to 3-5 containers a week. When the bookings hit double digits a week , I could not ignore it anymore. I called Ms. Jones (with my heart racing) and I asked her what happened and were these legitimate bookings or was she double booking with us (a common practice in the shipping industry when a customer books with a "primary" carrier and a "secondary" one just in case the primary carrier is not able to perform).

Ms. Jones sighed and said that they were legitimate. Her tone was different. It was softer. She stated that while we did lose the RFP, when she booked with two titans of the industry (who had much lower pricing), they could not move the much needed containers to the Mexican location that they said they could. Why? Because their pricing was predicated on a "free flow" basis, that is to say, the containers were placed at the Mexican location by natural ebb and flow of containers and not done by active placement of the containers. Whereas the quote that I gave factored in active placement of containers to the Mexican location, hence the higher price!!

I saw the problem, through my inexperience, as one of pricing. And for all intents and purposes, so did the client, Ms. Jones! But it wasn't really about price, was it? It was about performance and, ultimately, about results. The pricing from the competitors was the key matter (at first) for Ms. Jones but as it became apparent that the containers were not being replaced every week to the Mexican site, then the pricing was a moot issue. Her need for a regular steady flow of containers (use value) outweighed any empirically lower price that the competition had to offer.

I learned a very valuable lesson as well and that was: how I saw the problem was the problem to overcome. If I saw the problem as pricing, then I would only address the problem as a pricing issue and not anything else. But the situation revealed a whole new different dynamic which was NOT related to pricing. That was an early epiphany.

Too many intelligent, sharp, insightful people in business look at their situation in flat one or two dimensions (product attributes and pricing). It is much like the saying "If all you have in the toolbox is a hammer, then all the world's problems are nails". It is a terrible shame because it robs them of a tool that cuts through a lot of the murkiness raised in transactions.

Proposition: How you see the problem is the problem. That is to say, if you see the problem as one of pricing or product-centered issue, then you limit the true nature of the problem and, in so doing, severely curtail your ability to solve the issue at hand due to this myopia.

In the sections yet to come, we will put price in its rightful context. I am not saying that it has no credence or bearing in business transactions. To say so is absurd, because it simply isn't true. What I am saying is that the premium we place on price (to the degree that it overrides many of other factors) is equally erroneous and misguided. That, ultimately, is the Price Fallacy. Because price can be used for many purposes:

A. To promote a hidden agenda as a filter by which to keep people out (as we will see in the next chapter)

B. To be used as a tool to promote the vendor mentality of some buyers

C. To be used as the final arbiter of who is most qualified – albeit mistakenly as demonstrated by the aforementioned Personal Case Citing

To disabuse yourself of the tyranny of the Price Fallacy is not easy. To do the same for the client is equally hard, if not harder. You can't "make" someone see that point of view by simply telling them that they are wrong to put such an emphasis on price. Instead, to diffuse the power of price, you must methodically and even subliminally take out the underpinnings of the power of price by creating a higher, overriding use value picture for your product, company and yourself to the potential client. Then, and only then, can the price dragon be slain. Then again, there are those who will NEVER see your point of view. You will find that out soon enough when you butt your head against obstinacy that cannot be explained or overcome.

So product isn't the key to success as it used to be. Neither is pricing. This strips most people of most of their "market" armor. This is a very scary place to be because the next question is: what can I offer to clients that they would want and choose over my other competitors?

Chapter 8:

Know Thy Client: What do Clients Really Want?

This is a question that all sellers or client facing professionals want to know - **What does my client really want?** Every client is different so that would depend on who you were talking about, but let's talk in general usable terms.

Of course one obvious answer is the product or service that is offered to either solve a problem or make their world better. But beyond the product's actual attributes, what else do they want?

Is it ease? Speed and timeliness? Accuracy? Quality? Or that old devil: price? What does anyone really want out of a business transaction? The specific needs of clients vary from person to person whether they are in the same firm or not. In the same person these needs may also change from moment to moment due to timing or other circumstances.

Criteria to Even Compete

If you are selling to a prospective client, there are several layers of consideration that you must hurdle to be successful in their mind:

For this demonstration, it is assumed that your product has a level of complexity and involves a higher cost or commitment (risk). That is to say, you are not selling toothpicks.

1. Are you even in the running to be a contender for the client's business by meeting the minimum product or service thresholds? If you are able to meet that requirement, you may continue onto the next hurdle.

2. How do you compare with the competition when it comes to the selection criteria (such as quality, timeliness, accuracy, price, specific features, etc.)? What is the importance or "weight" of each factor? This discovery is key to winning over the client.

3. If the differences of the other criteria are slight, the defining difference is usually price. If the client states that your price is too high compared

to the competition, does it mean that they can't afford you? Not usually so. They just don't want to pay more than they think they should. Why?

a. Because you are being perceived as being "equal" with what is out there.

b. They want to keep to a certain allotted budget.

c. They like to drive vendors down to the lowest number that they can achieve to hit internal metrics.

d. They are sadists who like to see vendors writhe in pain.

While the natural inclination is the last choice (which may be valid nonetheless), the others seem more probable. But what's wrong here?

If they can clearly afford your service but they don't see a real reason to spend for any differential between your product and that of others, you are left with a decision-tree scenario. Either the client can be guided to see that you do have "value" and that they are willing to accept and pay for it, or the client cannot.

Let's go down both branches of that decision tree:

Branch 1 of the Decision Tree:

*You **can** guide the client to see that you have use value*

You can satisfy both your needs and those of your client(s) if you can show them value enough to not only be selected, but also get as close to the price that you ask for.

The task is to demonstrate in the mind of the client that you bring enough value to be worthy of:

1. The prospective client giving you his business

2. Commanding the price that you have set for your product without any discounting

How does one accomplish these dual tasks? What is the catalyst to achieve the two aforementioned results? It comes down to the client's view or perception.

People, if they see value (perception), will prioritize, re-allocate, and re-budget for what they feel is important. Don't be self-deluding about this subject. No matter how "whiz bang" or "killer app" your product may be, if the client (buyer) doesn't see value in it, then all the "whiz bangs" become useless.

What then affects, or in this case enhances, the client's perception of what you have to offer? What is that elusive use value that everyone talks about but so few people attain? Consider this:

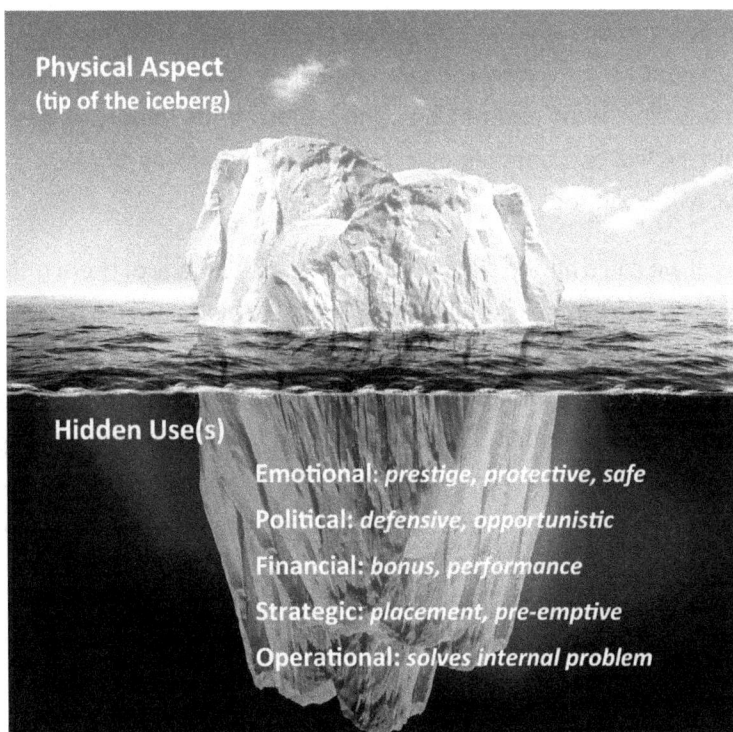

Physical Aspect
(tip of the iceberg)

Hidden Use(s)

Emotional: *prestige, protective, safe*

Political: *defensive, opportunistic*

Financial: *bonus, performance*

Strategic: *placement, pre-emptive*

Operational: *solves internal problem*

As with an iceberg, what you see is only the beginning of the story. What are usually visible (or made to be visible) are the physical or directly attributable aspects of the product/service to the need (expressed) at hand.

Hidden Use Values

To review: Use values of a product are the true uses or utility of the product as the client perceives it. In other words, the uses of the product, whether they be the actual physical product or other attributes that may fit into the buyer's paradigm, is what use values are all about. Use values are usually hidden from sellers for many reasons. The chief one would be so that you, as the seller, would not be able to manipulate that knowledge to your advantage.

Hidden use values are harder to detect and may be multi-faceted, but like an iceberg they may constitute the major impetus behind decisions. Hidden use values, by their nature, are seldom revealed. Here are some common ones:

Emotional Uses: A decision for one company over another may be based on the perception of ego. Often, decisions guised in "logical" clothing are actually very much driven by emotions such as arrogance, market retaliation, etc. In a lot of instances, decisions are driven by the need for safety. Many decisions are made to protect the "status quo" and not be controversial in its import. It has been said in certain circles, "no one has ever been fired for picking BLANK". BLANK could be IBM, Microsoft, etc.

Political Uses: If we could all add a dollar to our coffers for many of the acquisition decisions made in the business world that are driven by the internal politics of the company, then we would all be very rich indeed! The political decisions usually fall into one of two camps: one is of a defensive nature and the other is opportunistic. Whether a decision was meant to keep "territory" or expand them depends upon the situation; however, political reasons are at the root of a lot of corporate purchases, whether they be equipment, systems, or whole divisions/companies. The real efficacy of these decisions depends on time and results but the motivation is political.

Financial Uses: These uses may be to enhance the personal enrichment of the buyer or his/her department. Whether the buying decision will help to create results for a bigger bonus or increase the longevity of performance is usually well hidden.

Strategic Uses: This use may be mistaken for a political use but it actually deserves its own category. Higher level business managers (especially "C band" level) make decisions that have outcomes that may involve hundreds, thousands, or hundreds of thousands of people. So the ramifications are wide and deep. These decisions involve a lot of positioning for present and future health and performance. But even for lower echelon levels, the decisions to purchase or avail themselves of one company and its services over another may send "messages" to the market. These decisions may involve placement of the company in the market or may be done to pre-emptively prevent an event from happening. A departure from doing business with one company that has ALWAYS gotten the successful bid may be a signal of a change in management thinking of the vending company. The reverberations may send shock waves in the markets that are affected (whether by industry sector or by geography).

Operational Uses: The uses and applications of a product may solve an internal problem that the purchasing company doesn't really want others to know. The RFP for pre-employment vetting of new employees may come as a result of management realization that there is a high rate of employee theft or malfeasance issues that exist in the current employee pool. The RFP may be one of many steps which a company is using to clear the field and put in a fresh and untainted crew. Would this be something that you would ever see on the RFP specifications? Probably never.

Remember: it is critical to find out what your client's use values for your product, company and you are, whether they are readily visible or hidden!

So, how would it be if you were to receive an electronic RFP from a very large potential client and they made the following statement in their RFP:

This Request For Proposal is sent out to the market leaders in widgets and its ultimate purpose is to act as a legitimatizing exercise for the already arrived-at decision of retaining the incumbent company regardless of how good you or the other candidates may be.

Or how about this hypothetical RFP statement:

The company wishes to retain the services of a company for the main purpose of increasing the stature and esteem of the Chief Financial Officer. The winning candidate will be a market leader that will help not only in lowering costs and increasing efficiency but also in elevating the prominence of the CFO within the company and in the marketplace.

If these statements have raised a little smile on your face upon reading them, then great! However, if you were to read them in real life, then it would probably be profoundly shocking in its candor or cause dismay in its forthrightness. It is safe to say that these RFPs will never see the light of day! Yet there is always a story behind the story.

Uncovering Hidden Use Values is Important

How to get to the hidden use values is key to winning (or at least knowing when you don't have a ghost of a chance of winning). How do you not only map out these hidden use values, but also positively link what you and your product are to these attributes? Remember, we are not talking about the buying and selling of toothpicks. This is <u>not</u> a lower rated, unsophisticated product. Your product has a use value that is potentially <u>far greater than</u> the outwardly visible properties or capabilities that you would ascribe to it. Why is that? Because, when it comes down to it, you are looking at the product and its conventionally held uses – uses that the market has indicated to be of value – as just what is before you.

But truly, your product has a deeper and more specific use value in the context of the buying decision-maker's world. Use values that the client assigns to the product, your company, and you give it more or less importance than you would normally factor in. Mapping these use values and their level of importance (or weight) is key to knowing how to tailor your approach to the client. It is also crucial in determining the level of success you will enjoy with the client. Really, it is quite basic in principle. Once you "see" someone's use value for your product, you then can truly begin to focus in on them and address why they really are buying your product. The following illustration of my visit to an eyewear store will hopefully clarify my point on use values.

Personal Case Citing: My Trip to Lenscrafters

One day I finally had it with my sight! I realized that I needed glasses at the tender age of 46 years and so I went to get my eyes tested so I could get the right prescription for the right type of lens (trifocal was the prescription that the optometrist gave me). I then went to Lenscrafters and met an exceptional salesperson by the name of Michelle.

I went to the store with no major pre-conceived notion other than that I liked the look of Bulgari frames with my new prescription. I related my desire to Michelle who looked at me with a quizzical look on her face. When I noticed that she was looking at me in a strange way, Michelle said that I may want to re-think that notion over. I asked why and this is what transpired:

Michelle (M): "Why do you want Bulgari?"

John (J): "The styles are very sleek and I like that look a lot"

M: "I respect that; however, they don't fit your face. The frame's elbow doesn't clear your ear so they will tend to slip off."

J (crestfallen): "Oh."

M: "Might I ask what you want to do with your glasses or, in other words, what are you trying to achieve with them?"

J: "I want them to be functional, practical and professional looking."

M: "Okay, so you want them to be sharp looking and convey a certain look that makes people know that you are a thorough professional."

J: "Absolutely."

M: "Well, first of all, you need to have the frames' elbow go past your ear for better fit. Which is the first step toward conveying that look because you won't have to constantly push them up into place. Then you may want to go for more pragmatic colors such as black or dark brown which cements that professional look. Also, you'll need a progressive lens (no lines in the trifocal) so you can have a crisper look instead of all those lines that trifocals usually have. How do you feel about Varilux (the trifocal lenses that have wider range of vision)?"

J: "I like it."

M: "Good! Would you like photo sensitive lenses or sunglasses?"

J: "No. Anything else?"

M: "No, that is it. Try this frame based on what we talked about."

J: "Wow!! That's exactly the 'look' that I want to achieve! How much is this pair?"

M: "Much less than the ones you were thinking about and they are very strong. Let's fill out the order."

Did you see what happened? Michelle, in a very short amount of time and with limited questioning, got to what I wanted:

"Functional"

"Practical"

"Professional looking"

And more importantly, what the use values were that belied these characteristics:

"Functional" = no fuss, little maintenance yet having all the capabilities that modern lenses have to offer

"Practical" = not expensive, resilient

"Professional looking" = muted yet sharp, no distractive lines, creating a crisp image

Now overlay these use values with attributes of the lenses and frames that addresses the use values' implications:

"Functional" = no fuss (frames that fit the face), little maintenance yet having all the capabilities that modern lenses have to offer (Varilux)

"Practical" = not expensive (much less in price), resilient (strong)

"Professional looking" = muted yet sharp (black or dark brown), creating a crisp image (progressive lenses)

In a very short amount of time, Michelle was able to cut to the core of not only what I was using the glasses for (in all of its physical characteristics) but also what the hidden use values of the glasses, such as creating a crisp, professional image that had very little fuss and was strong.

In theory it sounds so easy, but there are many obstacles to this type of visibility. One of the main impediments may be the disconnection between what the client outwardly espouses as his needs versus what his real and hidden needs are. It may be that some companies purposely use "smoke screens" to hide their true agendas or, as is the case for most firms, conflicting camps or ideas are at work to create a labyrinth of needs and agendas that obscure the true agenda items behind any buying decision.

Proposition: The USE of a product or service usually transcends the physical nature of the product itself. That is to say, there are many powerful and potent use values embedded in you, your company and your product/service that you may not be aware of. However, once you find them out, then these are powerful tools at your disposal.

But to gain access to what the client truly values in terms of uses, you must be afforded the opportunity and visibility to do so. It then comes down to a question of: what kind of a relationship do you have (or want) with the client?

Vendor Versus Vending Partner

Are you a "vendor" or a "vending partner"? Some characteristic distinctions between the two are shown below:

Vendor	Vending Partner
Reactive	Proactive
Price, feature driven	Trust driven
Client offers innovation	Partners work together to innovate
No visibility into client's world	Knowledge of and interest in client's world
Formal channels emphasized	Informal channels utilized
Client doesn't solicit advice	Client asks for guidance
No ability/interest in new projects	Constantly create new growth opportunities
Very little interaction	Continuous interaction (informal & formal)
Working on low to mid levels on the management continuum	Working at highest levels on the management continuum

To have the opportunity to know what the client truly values in terms of uses would come more naturally from the vending partner relationship than from a simple vendor relationship.

If you chose the vending partner relationship (which you should for optimal performance), then you must position yourself into that role. It doesn't come by accident and it certainly doesn't come by following pre-established "vendor" rules that a lot of companies espouse. It does come through careful design and a purposeful endeavor to break down barriers to establish a truly great working relationship.

Ultimately, it is the type of relationship that you have with the client (which you can help to shape in a very big way) that determines if the client will allow himself or herself to see the use value of your product, your company and finally you.

But what if the client doesn't see use value in what you have to offer? Then what? And why?

Branch 2 of the Decision Tree:
*You **cannot** guide the client to see that you have use value*

This could be the result of different factors:

1. You were unsuccessful in establishing your product's use value in the mind of the potential client, or it was not strong enough to overcome other messages or obstacles.

2. The client has no compelling reason to change and include you in the mix of vending partners

3. The client is prevented from making changes due to legal or contractual obligations, or political reasons.

For whatever reason, sometimes you cannot get your point through. It happens to the very best of us who sell. Know that you cannot win all battles and that there are some situations or people/organizations that are positioned in such a way that you may not get through.

But what if, in your dealings with a potential new client, you encounter a client or organization that falls under two very different categories:

Category 1

A potential client who intentionally does not want to have you become his or her vending partner. Whether it is because they see no need or they would like to keep the status quo, you are not going to reach them no matter how well you have positioned yourself. Even the so called "equalizers" such as requests for proposal (RFPs) can be and are, in some cases, used to mask hidden agendas of preferential treatment. Do you think that this will ever be said to you in the open? Probably not.

Right about now you might be saying – is this for real? Do some companies purposely use sieves to block out certain vendors and let others in? The answer is unfortunately, yes, this does occur. You will probably not see any documentation on this issue but anecdotally there are enough examples culled in everyone's experience to give concern about this scenario.

This isn't sour grapes. Remember, this line of thinking is predicated on the assumption that your product is good enough to be considered in the running. So it isn't a matter of performance; it is a matter of "uses" or value perceptions that are derived from the selected vendor and their product. And, in the case of a company that purposely "stacks the deck" but will not reveal that fact, it becomes nearly impossible to know that you were never going to win their business.

Personal Case Citing – When Relationship Takes Precedence

There are two cases that I would like to cite for this section -- one that I knew about but was not involved in (the first case) and one that I was involved in directly (second case).

Case 1:

A global fast food restaurant giant had a RFP bid that asked all the top security (guarding) firms to participate for some of their key US assets. This would be not only a very prestigious piece of work for whomever won the award but also had a possibility of growing the business even more (much more) due to the size of the potential client.

Nate, one of the top salesmen of the parent company I worked for, put in for the bid on behalf of our company. The pricing, logistics, documentation and everything that would go into the RFP were put into place with a lot of care. Nate had some guidance (prior to the RFP) from the global security director, Don, as to how this monolithic company operated and what their pet peeves were so that Nate had a pretty good idea of what kind of work was expected of our company.

After many hard weeks of work, the RFP was submitted and the going over of the numbers and deliberations by the potential client was the next thing to happen. After a certain time, the RFP results came back and the result was that our company won the bid! Nate was ecstatic! Don stated that all that was left was to do some finalization of paperwork and then they would transition over to our company in terms of the guarding. Nate was busy getting the logistics of transition ready with the operations team. This was a major coup!

A short time later, not too much later, Nate got a call from Don. Don sounded disgusted and unhappy. Don told Nate that there had been a change in plans (which was well within their legal rights to do so) and that our company was not the winner but rather a small footprint company was chosen. Nate could not believe his ears! What? Why? Don was just as upset as Nate. However, the decision came from a much higher pay grade than his and Don had to abide by the decision.

Fast forward a year later. I was talking to Don and asked why he left the monolithic fast food giant and he said that he had had it with being overridden by upper management based on politics. I asked him what he meant by that and he said (in a very candid moment) that the decision really had gone to my company; however, one of the board of directors prevailed upon Don's boss to make the call in favor of this small footprint company. It turned out to be that the director had ties to the small footprint company and leveraged his position to change the decision.

Case 2:

My team was bidding for an executive protection detail RFP that came out of a major broadcasting company. The work was a very extensive protection detail and the rate of return was very positive due to the large number of hours entailed. We worked like dogs to get the RFP response in with the utmost amount of professionalism and care. The comments during the selection committee vetting were very positive about our response. Even the normally stoic procurement manager stated that he was very impressed and he asked questions of an operational nature that pointed to the possibility that we would be engaged to do the work very quickly. When the award notice came out, we were told that we did not win. A local firm had won. While it was disappointing, we moved on.

A few weeks later, we got a call from the number two security person who knew the head of our operational unit and he was calling to complain about the winner of the RFP award. In the process of his commiseration, he revealed that the owner of the winning firm <u>had very strong relationship</u> with his boss (who was the major decision maker).

In a post script note, it was a form of irony that the copious amount of hours that was touted during the RFP process had shrunk dramatically due to the worsening economic circumstances of 2008.

Category 2

A potential client who truly treats their vendors in such a way as to de-personalize the transaction and buying decisions to create "maximum efficiencies". This type of client likes to keep everyone at an arm's length distance from themselves. They do not like to share any information because to do so would diminish their control.

Their use values is very quantifiable, and as such they pick their vendors based on pre-determined metrics. If you are, say, the lowest bidder that can create units at an output that is consistent and of a certain quality, then you will probably have a piece of their business. However, usually attendant to this scenario is that the margins for this kind of business are low (either because of the client or the competition) and as a result you as the seller must make the decision of whether or not to pursue this client.

If you do, fine, but as is the way with almost all these types of relationships, they lend themselves very easily to swapping out of vendors should one (or some) not work out. The level of participation that you will enjoy in knowing them and helping them achieve their business goals will be limited, if non-existent.

Proposition: In the absence of a successful mapping and addressing of the buyer's hidden "uses" by the seller, the emphasis of the client will be to dwell on "externals" such as product, attributes, pricing, etc.

Even though these two scenarios are vastly different, the problem they present is not. The question is whether you, as the seller or client-facing professional, are willing to pursue these clients. The first scenario (a.) has a hidden agenda and so is harder to diagnose as to whether the efforts expended to attain their business would be better off directed toward someone else. The second scenario (b.) is a lot more overt in its behavior and agenda items. Both, however, tend to shut off communication at anything more than a cursory or elementary level. If, even with your best attempts, you are not able to penetrate beyond the most basic level, then you may want to re-consider if these clients are worth the pursuit.

Crossroads with a Client

So, what is the defining difference that will allow you to be successful with a client versus failing with them? This is where you have to do two things in order to achieve success at grasping what the client wants.

First, re-think the way you look at your product and what you have to offer. "Oh, is that all" you may be thinking but I am very serious about this. Earlier we said "how you see the problem is the problem" but now we must consider "how you see the product is the product".

Second, do the necessary homework, uncover and establish the use values of the client firmly in your mind and address those use values based upon what you have to offer as a product, person and company.

Chapter 9:
Emergence of The Honorable Relationship

Like the song says, "Everything old is new again". It seems as if everyone is jumping on the "relationship" bandwagon, especially if you listen in on interviews for positions ranging from sales directorships to marketing analysts to brand managers. "How to use" relationships, "when to leverage" relationships, blah, blah, blah, blah, blah.....

If it sounds trite and overused after the third hearing, then it probably is. In fact, it is a new window dressing of the same drab house of colloquialisms. The word "relationship" has replaced "listening", "needs/benefit", "client focused" and other such mantras in the popular vernacular much like "solutions" has replaced "answers" and "skill sets" has replaced "capabilities". Yet, to avoid throwing out the baby with the bathwater, one must consider the true underlying meaning of relationships and the power that they are invested in by the participants.

Someone once said that "the Relationship is the Contract", and when I heard that, I knew I was experiencing an epiphany! Here was the distillation of many arduous years of work and experience in a simple yet powerful phrase. That was when the wheels started to turn as to the clear and present truth that lay before our very eyes! It was this: Relationships – not systems, not pricing, not "killer apps", not master service agreements, not any of that but simple and rock solid relationships was not only the glue that bound but was the engine that kept companies (monolithic or small) and nations together and humming. Forget about contrived "networking", manufactured "events" and talks of "synergy" – it has always been, is now, and always will be about: RELATIONSHIPS.

But as I thought further, I realized it wasn't just <u>any</u> relationship that was successful but it was the ones that were based on understanding, competency, respect, credibility, trust, innovation, and growth. In short, it was a relationship based on high integrity -- an "honorable relationship". And if you dissect the previous sentence, you will find in it a classic progression of a good relationship:

<u>Understanding</u> each other and being <u>competent</u> on both sides helps foster an environment that gets things done. This mutual effort (over time) breeds <u>credibility</u>, and with experience, credibility morphs into a wonderful thing called

trust. Trust, once established and maintained, will nurture <u>innovation</u> and further <u>growth.</u>

The Honorable Relationship is not new. It is a model patterned after personal and professional rules of conduct that are older than recorded history. The way it is carried out may be entrenched in the 21st century, but the core of it is drawn from a very old and primal code of conduct in doing business, especially old world cultures (Europe, Asia, Middle Eastern, African, etc.). So it pre-dates the "classic" sales approach by millennia.

Let me disabuse you of any wrong notions at this juncture. The Honorable Relationship is not based on "warm and fuzzy" feelings, or using one's interpersonal skills (though they do help) but rather an honorable relationship is based on a platform built by all the above stated attributes. The platform once built and properly maintained will last beyond fiscal cycles, years, decades and help both sides to reap manifold "fruit".

The goal of **The Honorable Relationship** program is to bring your interactions with your client to a whole new level – a better, stronger and more effective level. It will minimize or eliminate most of the business concerns enumerated by hinging your competitive advantage on the strengths of your client relationships. (Of course, the given underlying assumption is that you are within a price competitive zone and provide high-quality services and/or products. If you don't have these two, then no matter what you do will fail anyway.)

These relationships (both external and internal) are the backbone which support everyone involved. They are natural, symbiotic partnerships that cut through time, culture, industry, and circumstance. <u>You will understand that your role is as vital as the client's</u>. This should be made clear from the very beginning of any business transaction, and steadily reinforced as the relationship progresses.

You will also see that your company must be fully engaged with the client in a manner that conveys competence, confidence, discernment, and a willingness to innovate. Learning to assess your situation is vital. You must look at your company, your competition, your market, and your existing as well as future clients. What are your business "sales" based on? Product, performance, convenience, friendship, contracts?

The goal of The Honorable Relationship is to help you realize that your true and ultimate "competitive advantage" lies in the relationships you will establish with your clients, and that all else is prone to being overtaken by the competition.

In short, you must be willing to take off the glasses that you have been wearing to perceive the world in which you inhabit and put on a new pair of lenses. These lenses look at people as multifaceted and complex individuals, and not as units (and that includes your own self-perception in the context of the business world). This lens also perceives that business relationships (while not altruistic) are not zero sum gain propositions in which if I win, then you must lose (or vice versa).

This lens also sees business transactions not as transference of resources between two or more parties but rather the culmination and tangible manifestation of the relationships that you and your client have established.

What is required is a total worldview reformation in your own mind and nothing short of it will work. **This is critical to exorcizing the same old tired patterns of thinking and conduct that you have become accustomed to. It is the first key step to creating a very effective philosophy, strategy, and operational mindset that is uniquely your own.**

In other words, it is time for you to open your eyes to a MUCH BIGGER WORLD than you could've imagined! You do not have the same old tools and thinking anymore, and that is a good thing! But what you do have are many more options and avenues of creating a business relationship than ever before. In fact, they are all different because each personal dynamic that you encounter with a new client is different than any other you've had. It has to be this way or else it is not real and the exercise of client-facing work becomes disingenuous and rote.

This may be somewhat scary to some of you because there is no set pattern as to how these relationships are conducted. There is no repetitive road map that neatly shows how these personal dynamics play out. That may seem daunting but in reality it is a good thing primarily for two reasons:

1. It allows the spirit of innovation and iteration to take place which can only lead to incredible creativity.

2. It helps you to stay fresh, crisp and sharp because there is no complacency of sameness.

But just because there is no set template for how these relationships play out does not mean there are no traits that these positive relationships exhibit. And it certainly does not mean that there aren't some templates in which to help setup and foster these relationships. That is specifically what we will address for the balance of this book – the template for establishing a relationship that is extremely effective in serving both parties' needs (yours and the clients) and forging a very strong bond in the process!

Case Citing: The mystery of the Jewish shipper

When I was just starting out in the logistics industry, I was working for a classic container line company. In my travels for the company, I found myself having dinner at a restaurant in Rotterdam with two old hands at the game of transportation.

As the evening went on, one of them told a very interesting story about a very powerful Jewish Dutch magnate that shipped his company's products all over the world. This powerful magnate gave ALL of his business to this one particular local Dutch freight forwarding company to ship all his goods around the globe. The Dutch forwarding company that enjoyed this business received thousands upon thousands of container loads worth of business from the Jewish magnate but for no obvious, explainable reason. The Dutch forwarding company had no real "killer network" that made him more efficient, no tiered pricing that made him cheaper and no real advantage over any of the huge competitors that were vying for the magnate's business.

In fact, the major freight forwarding companies of the world and the global shipping lines were all trying to pull the magnate's business away from the small local Dutch freight forwarder but to no avail. They flew in very powerful executives to talk him out of doing business with the local Dutch forwarder and start doing business with them. They enticed the magnate with all sorts of incentives and programs but the Jewish tycoon didn't budge not by one inch. No part of his business was going to anyone other than this local Dutch forwarder.

---

cont'd

Was it nationalism, thought the suitors. Nope, even the other Dutch local entities did not get any of his business. Could they go through the Jewish angle? Not at all because the head of the local Dutch forwarder was clearly Gentile. What was it then? The suitors were stymied.

Years later, the truth came out. The reason why the Dutch Jewish tycoon gave his business solely to the Dutch forwarding company was because during World War II with his whole family shipped off to Nazi concentration camps, the Jewish tycoon (who was then an adolescent) sought and received shelter and a hiding place by a kindly Dutch Gentile family that he knew. The young Jewish boy was so grateful for their act of love and heroism that he vowed he would repay their kindness someday somehow.

Later in life, the Jewish boy grew to be a successful businessman and sought out the Dutch family only to find out that one of the sons of the family was the head of the small freight forwarding company. Ever since then, the Jewish magnate made good his vow by shipping everything through the Dutch freight forwarding company owned by the scion of the family that saved him.

Why did I put this story in here at this point of the book? Because I wanted to illustrate the power of a very strong, honorable relationship. The realist (or cynic) among you may say "Well, it would be wonderful if my family could've saved my biggest client's life many years ago, but they didn't." But that dismissal of this story misses the point. It wasn't what happened to create the relationship but rather the power of the relationship that helped to transcend all influences such as competitors, markets, and the vagaries of this world.

You don't have to save someone from death or fight a war alongside a comrade or be related to a person in order to enjoy that type of relationship. In fact, I have known people that have had some type of experience or connection similar to the aforementioned situations and STILL NOT have a business relationship at all. It is about establishing that kind of relationship that this book is laser-beam focused on. This story may be a very dramatic, stark allegory of the power of a relationship but it underscores what can be achieved. What you can achieve.

Section Two:
The Strategies of the Honorable Relationship

The Honorable Relationship is a unified and integrated approach; a new way of looking, thinking and pursuing business ventures in terms of the revenue production process based on rock solid historical precedence and human predilections. This philosophy and methodology is based upon the relationship dynamics forged between you, your company, and that of the client and their various constituents.

The question now is: How do you start an Honorable Relationship? What are the necessary steps to be taken that will begin to utilize the power of this timeless yet somewhat displaced way of doing things? Much like a master builder, you must build a firm foundation; a foundation as free of the "old" type of thinking that you were laboring under as much as possible; a foundation that is built one brick at a time.

Chapter 10:
World Domination Program

I like to be dramatic. But in light of what we are talking about -- the position that you occupy in the business world -- why not look at it as a personal world domination plan? As I am prone to say – if you are going to be a bear, be a grizzly!

Mapping out a strategy is the first step in any plan for world conquest, even benevolent ones. And (as with all world conquests plans) it must:

- Employ the battle landscapes involved in the warfare

- Consider the resources (people, time, material) that it takes to wage the campaign

- Be fairly simple yet nuanced to anticipate contingencies

- Be effective regardless of culture, location, changing events, etc.

In summary, a "world domination" strategy must use and rely on ALL of the resources at your disposal. That is why this section is separated into two parts: Internal and External Honorable Relationships.

The first part (Internal Honorable Relationships) covers the assessment and usage of resources available within your company and/or its affiliates and subsidiaries. This is vital because, in order for you to pursue vigorous and sustainable revenue production, you must have the material to prosecute it. What material? Operational infrastructure, product, pricing, company support and people willing to support your initiative to win.

After marshaling all your resources into a coherent effort internally, the task turns to external matters. The External Honorable Relationships section covers ways in which you can position yourself and your company into a space that is highly coveted: one in which not only will you receive business from your clients, but also one that they seek your counsel and put you on the top of their Rolodex or call list. You become as the psychologists call a "referent power" because you will have their ear and trust. This position is not easy to attain; however, it is well worth the effort once attained.

So let's get started.

Internal Strategy

Time for some self-assessment and contemplation of what assets you have within you and your company's arsenal of resources that can be utilized for market domination.

1.   Company's reputation and image

2.   Company's products and services

3.   Company's internal and external support mechanisms

4.   Company's people

5.   Your own personal reputation and image

6.   Your talents and capabilities

These are key considerations but one that has a myriad of answers based on you, your company and your products' position in the world.

Company's Reputation and Image

How does your company perceive itself in the market spaces in which it operates? Does it look at itself as the lowest priced and most affordable choice amongst the various purveyors of products/services? Or does it perceive itself as the middle-of-the-road brand neither being the very best nor the worst in terms of quality and/or pricing? Or does your brand fight aggressively to be the "best" in category?

It is very important to take this into consideration because it will very difficult to inculcate yourself to your client in the manner proscribed by this book if your firm perceives itself at the lower end of the food chain. The methodology proposed in this book can still be used but will not be as successful as a situation wherein the company is not undermining your message of branding and non-reliance on pricing as a basis by which you enjoy a client's patronage.

If your company's overall image is poor in quality, then you may want to re-examine if the Honorable Relationship approach is appropriate in light of the reality that may be too hard to overcome. Or you may want to re-examine employment with them.

Company's Products and Services

How do the company's products and/or services stack up with that of the competition's? Specifically, does the technical and physical product of your company roughly approximate that of the competition's products' capabilities? If so, then that is a good starting point. It doesn't have to be necessarily superior to that of the competition, but it may have aspects that are more desirable than others.

If there is a wide gap in performance between your company's products and that of the competition, then you may have a harder time trying to overcome this. However, this situation is more "fixable" than if your company's reputation/ image or self view is of a lower caliber (and your company is okay with that scenario).

Company's Internal and External Support Mechanisms

You can tell a lot about a firm (even your own) by the company it keeps. Are there suppliers, partners or peripheral industry sources that you can leverage for help in penetrating clients? Do they have inroads that you may not otherwise be able to have? Specifically, are there legacy relationships that these folks may already have in place that may be used so as to gain further penetration than previously thought possible?

Sometimes market intelligence from key people in these entities can be very helpful in guidance of what works or doesn't work. Firms or persons that have done work with targeted clients are able to give you a foreshadowing of things to come, including what to avoid or to accentuate.

Associations of the industries that your company occupies or that of the target client are also very helpful in getting valuable intelligence or being the connective bridges to key individuals within the firm that you are seeking to do business with.

The power of associations must not be underestimated. They are the gatekeepers in keeping people out but they can be very powerful influencers if you are able to co-opt them in your revenue production work. We will cover this more in depth in a later section called The Effect of Multiples.

Company's People

An Honorable Relationship should exist internally as well as externally. If you don't have strong internal relationships in place prior to client engagement, how will you know operational deployment and delivery will be there when you need it? It is vital to harness the collective power of a team's talents, competencies, intellect, and connective relationships to be able to approach the targeted clients and markets with such an overwhelming force that it would be hard for any to oppose your efforts.

How is this to be done? There are certain things you can assess about your firm and even certain things you can do, internally, to get things into place so as to effectively use the resources your company already possesses.

Internally Driven Aspects:

1. Co-opting those within the company to help carry out your vision. Buy-in from key operational or corporate people is very important. Without it, you would not be able to achieve any kind of results.

2. Using or working around WIIFM (What's In It For Me?) mentality. Discernment of the various "triggers" of the associates you work with, help to align what you are trying to do in the marketplace with that of the individual's goals within your firm so that there is a direct correlation. This makes helping you much easier. Is it prestige? A need to win? Pursuit for recognition? What are some drivers that make people really respond? Tap it and direct it.

3. Knowing your way around your organization – how to co-opt help from areas that you least expect. What I mean by this is that your organization (any organization) has a cast of characters that is rich with potential to help you "bag" the big animals. Some of these folks are not necessarily the most helpful from the outset.

Personal Case Citing: Befriending the "Enemy"

I once worked at a container ship company that had a very tenured and union driven shop. I was viewed as "management" and so there was an automatic layer of friction and a certain amount of distrust on both sides. I was working hard to win over a potential new client but it required routing that was quite unusual for the containers (instead of putting them on a container ship in Seattle so that they would eventually end up in Europe). The client wanted us to rail them over with the cost of that move to be factored in which, in theory was fine; however, the rail moves required a lot of containers to be spotted (dropped off) at the client's facility in Redmond, Washington (no, the client is not who you think it may be judging from the location)!

The proposed move also had the added headache of involving the railroad cutoff schedules, and that is never an easy coordination. The operations manager, Turner, was never known as being easy to get along with by most people's reckoning and he had a long tenure and the respect of management behind him. Turner was also not a boat rocker (no pun intended) by backing up hare-brained schemes of newbie account executives such as yours truly in my quest to build a reputation as a dealmaker.

Yet, I needed Turner's buy-in into the plan for it to work or else it would not be able to be implemented.

I took a deep breath and met with Turner to discuss my plans and seeking his support.

John (J): "Turner, I need your help on this new proposal for Client X and I was wondering if you looked at my email on it?"

Turner (T): "Yes I did and I gotta say that I don't think it will work!"

J: "Why not?"

T: "It's too much work and a nightmare to keep straight."

J (getting angry): "Since when is not doing something just because it is hard a good and valid reason?"

T (tensing up): " Listen kid, I've been doing this as many years as you've been alive and doing stuff twice as hard as what you propose so don't go down that road. You won't win!"

J (apologetic): "Alright. I am sorry to offend you. Turner, what I am trying to do is to get this new client that could give us a huge amount of business and I need your help."

T: "John, you don't understand. Let's say you get this client and we get a boatload of new business., You will have moved on but me and my crew will be stuck working this mother till one day we screw up (due to Murphy's law) and then I get yelled at!"

J (resigned): "Turner"

T: "What?"

J: "I misunderstood you and your team. I was told that you have a great team that can do a lot of things. In fact, the reputation is that there's not much you can't do. But I see that I was mistaken."

T: "I know what you are doing, so get off it! You aren't going to shame me into doing something."

J: " No actually. I am trying to find out if you have any pride in what you do and in this company."

T: "Of course I do."

J: "Well, if you do, then it seems odd to me that you wouldn't work with me to flex our muscles and show the client and our management what you and your boys can really do? Yes, this move is challenging and fraught with a lot of missteps because it is very complicated, but if you carried it off, then talk about point of pride! You are the only one who could do this, that's why I came here. And, you may not believe this, but I will not just move on, I will work with you and the client to get this done right. You aren't the only one who is going to do this."

Turner looked at me and started to smile. He said "I need this like I need a kick in the head!"

Even though he probably thought what I said was hokum, Turner was intrigued as to how this move would work in actuality. He then set out to work on the rough plans to move all this freight. We had numerous conversations after that day and with each call the adamant "NO" became "maybe" to finally "yes".

EPILOGUE: The rail move was planned as thoroughly as a moon shot and Turner and his crew pulled off the logistical nightmare of moving 50 containers a week with various destinations and routings FLAWLESSLY! The client was overjoyed and our company gained a great reputation as a "can do" company because nobody had even dared thought of doing such an audacious move. It was all because of the genius and tenacity of crusty Turner and his dogged team of miracle workers.

So, different people have different triggers but in order to utilize people's talents and skills at their best and highest use, you really have to discover those triggers.

---

4. Creating "cell" units within the organization that will work with you. I know that "cell" units has a bad connotation in this day and age because whenever the term is invoked, it invariably is in the context of a terroristic group. But really there is a reason for the success of cell groups. They are small (therefore, communication is direct and simple);, they are of various skills/backgrounds (lending various types of expertise to solving a problem); and they are very laser-beam focused on the task at hand.

The creation of an informal band of co-workers from disparate departments to come together to work on a client or solve a problem is when a company works at its best. If you are privileged to be able to work with various cell teams (separated by geography or functional lines), then you'll really see how they may work to go on the issues at hand. You may also be the connective link between these cell units to work together on "blue sky" projects or monolithic clients.

In a Personal Case Citing coming up in the Client Champion section, there is a highlighting of the power of what a great cell team can do.

Your own personal reputation and image

Let us take stock of your own reputation and market image. This may be difficult because it is very hard to leave your own skin and examine yourself through the lens of another. However painful or difficult as this may be, it is an exercise that is vital for you to understand the pitfalls and strengths that you have developed as a result of your tenure in the business world and the market space that you (personally) occupy.

The best way to get a TRUE assessment is to talk to the ones that must interact with you. These folks populate your workaday world and will give you the perspectives that you need. Who are these "angels of our better nature"? They are as follows:

- Clients (the core folks – not necessarily the ones you are buddies with)

- Your co-workers (superiors, peers and subordinates – yes, even the administrative staff)

- Your channel partners (the market inhabitants that work with you to prosecute your work)

- Your spouse (the most honest critic really)

What, ultimately, is to be gotten from querying these people? It is to get a level set of where you are currently versus where you aspire to be. Sometimes we think we are already "there" but find out in a very rude way that this is simply not the case. What would you ask of these people? Here are some guiding questions that may get you started.

Questions to pose to the folks that know you best:

- What do I excel in doing? Punctuality? Accuracy? Delivery? Coordination? Mediation? Persuasion?

- Use four adjectives to describe me or my business persona

- What are my weaknesses or shortcomings – give me four examples

- Advise me of two things that I need to immediately do better or eliminate from my way of doing business

- What do you think that I think of you? That is to say, how do you think I perceive you?

- What is my greatest value to you?

Kind of different questions, aren't they? Not necessarily business related but oh so relevant to the heart of how you are to conduct yourself in this world. This is part of the process you need to take to perfect your approach to the business world.

Be warned, some of the answers may not be pleasant to hear. Especially the comments made by the ones that are very close to you. That is alright because that's how any of us really learn from others.

There are reasons why you are at the level you are and maybe, if you are really honest with yourself, these difficult things that you will hear will reveal the real reasons as to why you've not achieved the next level of performance or refinement.

Address these comments with grace and acceptance to change. If you try to dismiss them or rationalize them away ascribing flaws to those that have critiqued you, then you really have missed the point of the whole book. Diminishment of critiques by those closest to you only prolongs your time in the wilderness of self-disillusionment.

Finally, while the process of exfoliating yourself of bad habits and flawed behavior/ thinking is painful, the endeavor is very much worth it for you to change for the better. Recognition of these blemishes and the commitment to change them are the first steps to a better way.

Your talents and capabilities

What is in your personal toolbox? This may be an assessment of: native skills (language, cognitive powers such as mathematics, "business sense"), knowledge/ education (specialized education or experiences), or physical/emotional/mental capabilities. Assess what you have to offer as a person in totality in the pursuit of your business aims.

Many people really submerge some of their best talents and skills in their regular, workaday world -- characteristics such as sense of humor, writing or speaking facility, an ability to accurately "read" others using their God-given instinctual radar, a vision of where to go or pursue certain business endeavors based on experience and intuition, etc. It is a criminal shame to not harness these rich gifts.

Take time to assess these skills and refine them as well. It is a good thing to be able to use different skills and talents that you've not used before. If you tend to be more verbal, then work on your writing skills. In doing so you'll find that it will improve your speaking and presentation skills.

It is important NOT to neglect the internal strategy and resources that you will need to get you the desired goals of your business, because, in thinking upon and integrating the internal strategy with that of your external strategy, you can have alignment of planning and execution.

External Strategy

Pursuing an Honorable Relationship with your client requires effective tools that will forge and sustain a long-lasting and profitable partnership. The following is a roadmap of where the upcoming chapters of this book will take us. Remember, Knowledge leads to Understanding Use Value which leads to Relationship which ultimately leads to Exploration (Growth).

A Template for Success:

1. KNOWLEDGE
   Homework
   Leveraging the Power of Multiples
   - The role of core accounts
   - The role of WIP (Work in Progress) accounts
   - The role of industry groups and/or associations

   Aim and Shoot High
   Client Champions
   Getting Sticky With It!

2. UNDERSTANDING USE VALUE (in Real Life Situations)
   What is the Client Really Saying? Questions to Ask and Answers to Listen For
   - The Real Role of Procurement
   - The Truth About Contracts

3. RELATIONSHIP
   Following a Series of Permissions
   What is a Brand?
   Creating Your Own Personal Brand

4. EXPLORATION
   Leadership Vortex
   Stewardship Compact

In the immortal words of Jackie Gleason "...and a way we go!"

Sub Section: KNOWLEDGE

Chapter 11:
Homework

Understanding a client is not an easy task. It requires a fair amount of work and diligence that lasts throughout the relationship. However, in the beginning, the most amount of work needs to be expended to get past the human and organizational hurdles. To do so requires homework to be done even prior to meeting a client.

How much do you really know about the potential client? How can you impress them that you are worth doing business with? It really comes down to credibility and competence. While everyone may say that they are both, the trick is to inform the client of your credibility and competence WITHOUT saying so. This comes from doing your due diligence on the client and their industry.

Nowadays with the preponderance of information-gathering tools, there really is no excuse to not doing homework on a client prior to calling them. There are databases, search engines, social network sites, statistics-gathering services, libraries, and a host of other sources that can help you in doing research.

This plethora of sources has been a boon to anyone who does sales or account management. However, one must direct this information searching wisely. What do you want to know about the client? I usually start with the basics:

- Company and its subsidiaries (names, locations, heads)

- How old are they?

- What is the image or reputation of their company?

- What is their leadership known for?

- What industries do they occupy and what do they make?

- How do they make or market their product (rough outline as to the process)?

- How big are they in terms of revenue, market share or employee population?

- What is their ranking in the market or industry they occupy?

- What are some recent headlines or newsworthy changes?

- What is the word "on the street" about them (see next chapter on Leveraging the Power of Multiples)

- What is an interesting factoid about the company that you didn't know prior to research?

Why is the last question even on the list? Because it is AMAZING what you can learn (and in turn communicate to the client on a subliminal level) about a company from dropping a factoid into the conversation. Let me be more specific.

When you come into a meeting with an idea as to the depth, breadth, height, and makeup of a company, you've probably done more than most, if not all, of your competitors! This I have had re-affirmed to me by former and current clients again and again. They always cited that I tended to score better and thereby be viewed as more "professional" and "credible" because I did my homework on them. The extra factoid that stands out either about the client or the company draws interest (sometimes mildly, sometimes dramatically, as we shall soon see) but nonetheless the level of credentialing and discourse goes way up if you do the preparatory homework! There's no way to illustrate the point better than by citing four back-to-back personal case citings of when doing homework paid off.

Personal Case Citing: Breaking the Ice – A Simple Little Factoid

Prior to meeting (for the first time) Harold, the security director of a global staffing company, I did some noodling on the internet. What I found was the usual stats on company size, structure, span, etc. However I did run across a very interesting factoid of "Every minute of every business day, 312 people get placed by Company X" which was a claim that was made in one of their webpages. That struck me, so I wrote it down for my preparatory notes (the ones I bring when I see a client).

When I met with Harold, he seemed mannerly but a bit detached. Then I pulled out this little factoid of a gem in the middle of a conversation.

John (J): "You know, I've got to stop right here and say that in my research of your company, I found out that you folks place 312 people every minute of every business day."

Harold (H): "Where did you get that?"

J: "From one of your company's website."

H: "Hmmm, I didn't know that."

Epilogue: From that little encounter, it seemed his demeanor had changed. Harold became more invested in the conversation and covered a range of topics of which he was very forthcoming with the answers. Harold and I eventually ended up doing a risk assessment of their headquarters. Not a small project.

Personal Case Citing: Breaking the Ice – Making French Visitors Feel Welcomed

I was called to the Washington, D.C. area to do a presentation for a selection committee of a power company. This potential client was vetting my company (and others) to see who would do the due diligence (research on vending partners) work for them. I didn't know whom the specific competitors were but I knew that we were one of three finalists.

I was also told that the selection committee was partially comprised of a French contingency (three senior managers). I prepared by doing research on the power company and its French parent company. As I did research, I thought about what could tip my company to the positive side? Guessing that our competitors were probably all US companies and US citizens usually did not know a lot about French geography and culture (of which I count myself as one of the offenders), I made notes about their headquarters location and drew memories from my two previous business trips to Paris.

Day of the meeting and my associate and I were greeted in the DC suburb office of the company. We met the three US managers and the three senior French managers. As we started to unpack our laptops, I asked the French contingency of their trip over, how long they were going to stay and did they work out of the La Defense area of Paris. The lead French manager looked at me with a startled yet pleasant look on his face. "How do you know about La Defense?" he asked. "I know of it but I've never been there personally.

However, I have stayed in La Mirabeau and St. Michelle enclaves of Paris." I replied.

This then started a lively discussion in which we all talked about our individual experiences in Paris and in Europe. Now, it may seem a trivial opening formality but the group lightened up quickly. They didn't have their "selection committee" face on (which they had as we walked in) as much as amiable and agreeable looks afterwards. And guess what? We really did have a more convivial meeting throughout that morning.

Epilogue: We won the competition and went on to work with the client in a very friendly and professional manner.

Personal Case Citing: How Much Do You Know About Us?

The CFO of a potential client called me and asked me to meet with them on a very short notice basis. The company was a Broadway production company that had some concerns they wanted to address.

Due to the short turnaround time, I did some cursory research on the firm and went to the appointment. I met them at their office and we sat down with the CEO and CFO of the firm. When we got past the general pleasantries, the CEO asked a very direct question, "How much do you know about us?" He asked the question obviously to see if I (and my investigative company) really did know what we were doing and talking about. In replying, I began to tell him of his company's ownership of the number of theaters in US and Canada, that they just acquired a company recently, and how many productions they had on an average per year basis. As I was about to keep going, the CEO raised his hand and said to me, "You know us" very calmly and we then began to talk about what we could do for them.

Epilogue: We got the client's business and I am convinced that one reason that we did was because we proved to him that we knew his company and its world. It only makes sense in the context of the fact that they were hiring us for our ability to ferret out information.

Personal Case Citing: One in a Million Shot

My investigative company was in the running for a RFP (request for proposal) on a security matter by a global printer company. We had hurdled the earlier levels and now we were invited to present our case to the client in Paris. As a result, my team and I worked very hard to cover all the possible questions and scenarios.

In the act of preparing for the Paris meeting, I searched the internet for anything that I could find out about the potential client and this one division. I used various permutations of the company's name, division, discipline, and products. Nothing was grabbing me until I looked on the fourth page of Google many items down. Then what I saw totally rocked my world.

Ten items down on the fourth page, I saw a PDF file which pertained to the company so I opened the file. The first thing I saw was: "For Employee Eyes Only" on the top banner. This was no ordinary document! As I read on, the document covered sensitive information about the division and its products. It was breathtaking in terms of the scope of the document! I could scarcely believe such a document was in the public domain because it really should not have been.

Now I had to do some heavy contemplation. As I headed for Paris, my mind was weighing the benefits and the pitfalls of me revealing this information to the selection committee. It was risky but I felt it was the right thing to do.

During the meeting, during the middle of my presentation, I slid the document over to the main person on the selection committee, the program manager, Gregory. I said "Gregory, you may be interested in this document" as I transitioned between two slides.

Gregory's eyes became saucer-like when he read the document and then he started to scribble furiously on the margins of the document. He actually stopped paying attention to my presentation but that was fine with me. What I gave him was of incredible interest to him.

Finally, during a break in the session, Gregory could not contain himself any longer and pulled me aside and said "Man! Where did you get this document?" I said "the internet". Gregory's eyes got even wider (if that was possible) as he exclaimed "Oh no!" I then stated that is the type of work that my company did very well. We look for our client's weaknesses and we shine the light on them so that they can be remedied. With Gregory's knowing nod, I knew that this very simple message that I just delivered was backed up by a very powerful proof of that statement. The document took my statement out of the realm of "salesmanship" and into the realm of validation.

Epilogue: We won the RFP and I think that while there were probably many reasons for our win, the document was definitely the clincher in the mind of the main decision maker.

These personal case citings were presented not to underscore how great a salesperson I am but rather to emphasize the need to do homework on your prospective client. A little work upfront can make the difference between engagement or not. Truly.

Chapter 12:
Leveraging the Power of Multiples

"What multiples?" you may ask. The multiples of the multitude. Sorry, I didn't mean to sound like Dr. Seuss but there are people all around you that have the ability to help you if only you recognized that fact and knew how to channel that power towards achieving your goals!

There is an old rule that the great thinker Archimedes refined about the power of leveraging. The Archimeic rule (roughly stated) is if you put a fulcrum (usually a triangular object) under a long plank (like a seesaw) and you put a very heavy object on one plank end and a medium weight object on the other plank end; depending on where you move the fulcrum (usually towards the heavy weight) then it is conceivable to lift the much heavier object with medium weight object by sheer leveraging.

It was said that given the right leverage, you could lift the world.

Using the power of leveraging to do great tasks, you must consider what the lay of your business land is all about and the men and women that occupy that landscape. Earlier we reviewed that tapping into your own company's capable men/women has a very powerful effect in marshaling the forces to take on a project or client!

Now let's delve further the added benefits of leveraging others outside of your firm for information and

positioning. You can build new relationships faster, strengthen existing relationships, and achieve your goals more effectively by co-opting the talent and insight of the people around you, your client, and in the marketplace. Identify multipliers (people who can multiply your reach or knowledge) from these groups:

- Suppliers and Vendors

- Partners (Joint Ventures)

- Media

- Client's Competition

- Your Competition

- Former Employees of the Client (be very careful of content veracity and possibility of client's knowledge that you are talking to this group)

- Associations and Affiliations

NOTE: Anyone in the marketplace that services you or your client can be a multiplier.

What should you be seeking and who should you get it from? What you are looking for is knowledge of the client that gives insight into their world beyond the official or politically correct versions. Consider this: with so many people inhabiting a company and so many divergent thinking and agendas in any organization, it is fair to say that getting to the truth about a company's real structure, emphasis, hierarchy of power, agenda, etc. may not come from official organs such as website, annual reports, press releases, etc. Rather "the story behind the story" comes from people working in, with or around the client firm that you are targeting.

NOTE: The information gathered and the methods by which to do so MUST NOT be illegal or unethical. And the uses for the intelligence gathering is to further enhance your understanding of the client's world and not to have a malicious intent to misuse such information.

It is important to ask the "right" questions regarding the client pertaining to initiatives, state of contentment, undercurrents, the personality of the company and how it treats their constituents, areas of interest for the client company, people within the client company to consider or know as well as their attendant personalities/agendas/drivers etc. You are seeking information that falls into one of three buckets:

1. Validate or refute known information – things that you already know

2. Confirm or bring to light unknown knowledge – things you know that you didn't know

3. Revelatory knowledge – things you did not know that you did not know – unknowable information

The last one is the most tricky and the most rewarding in the sleuthing process to get at a client's true situation. There are certain initiatives or certain scenarios that only insiders or people that have some glimpses into these firms would know. This type of information is so new or secret or embedded into the client's world that all the Googling in the world will never get this information to come to the fore.

The line of questioning should be approached in a manner that I call ever tightening concentric circles. It is similar to how a shark attacks its prey . Sharks seldom (if ever) attack its intended meal straight on. Instead, the shark circles around the prey in odd shaped ellipses, taking swooping passes as it rubs against the prey. Why? It is gathering intelligence. When it comes close, it wants to know if you have anything to strike out against it. When it rubs against you, it wants to know your constitution – are you rough, scaly, tough, soft, spiny? Once it has determined that you are a choice victim that will not endanger the shark as it is about to devour you then guess what? It is too late!

Now, you are not a shark (at least hopefully you won't conduct yourself that way) but you do want to approach the client with ever tightening concentric circles. Whether you are reaching out to the client directly or to its satellite relationships, the purpose is to gather information. This information could come in the form of hard facts or soft data such as anecdotes, rumors or opinions. (See Exhibit 1 – Line of Questioning)

The reason for this important exercise is to allow your contact to provide:

- Information

- Introductions
- Insight into the client, their structures, and their environment
- Understanding internal "invisible" politics and power factions
- Personalities
- Budgets and timeframes
- Roadblocks

If these multipliers are inside a client firm, then they can also function as **client champions** and help build momentum for your initiative with the client. We will cover this in Chapter 14: Client Champions.

These multipliers can also give you a view of whether you want to do business with a company or individual...or not.

Multipliers not only offer insight but they also <u>may</u> help to make introductions to people who are influencers or decision makers. Influencers are people in or out of the client firm that have a powerful sway over the direct decision makers that you are trying to know and engage with.

Another form of using the power of multiples is one of using the knowledge derived from working with companies within same or similar industries which creates a multiplier effect in ramping up to be an expert. This requires approaching your clients (potential or current) in categories so as to benefit from knowledge that comes from aggregation. Let me be more specific. Let's say your business straddles many industries, such as security. Security is something that most, if not all, businesses need in one form or fashion. You can start with A for art museums to Z for zoos and every institution or business in between and find a need for security in one way or another. Now, if it does not seem practical to attack the market with a scatter-shot approach of getting anything that is out there, that is because it is not!

The key to success in market approach is to concentrate on two to three industries at the very most. If you find that your territory or region has a preponderance of banking, insurance and IT companies, then guess what? You just had the market show you what industries you may want to concentrate on. Either that or you can concentrate on the industries or companies that help to <u>support</u> banking, insurance or IT.

As you engage with, say, banking, you will find that the discussions tend to have a certain similarity from one banking entity to another. That makes sense because really a bank's issues or dynamics are fairly similar when it comes to security and, as such, a certain knowledge base is being developed as you proceed along discussions with these banking firms.

Same scenarios will emerge as you work with energy firms or IT firms. This type of multiplier applies to knowledge of industries and the specific dynamics that drive them.

A very powerful way of organizing your approach into the marketplace is as follows:

- **Core Accounts**

- **WIP Accounts**

- **Industry Groups/Associations**

The Role of Core Accounts

In order to be able to leverage (Archimedic rule) the knowledge that comes from knowing a particular industry or industries well, the usage of core accounts is key in establishing a base. Core accounts should represent no more than three industries and be of a certain size/stature that allows good business returns (but they do NOT have to be the industry leaders such as Walmart, Wells Fargo Bank, ExxonMobil for examples). Core accounts should be a list of 12 potential clients that represent winnable accounts in the following manner:

> **Banking:**
> Badda Bing Bank
> Fidelity To Us Corp.
> MyBank Inc.
> Sound Money Savings Bank

Insurance:
Accident Prone Co.
No Way 2 Pay Inc.
Banana Peel Reinsurance
SAFE (Slip and Fall Experts)

Information Technology (IT):
Techno Folks Corp.
Yabba Dabba Doo (hey, it could happen especially with the crazy technology company names you find)
Wonkie Inc.
Dude and Associates

Putting these companies into these industry "buckets" allows you to think along the lines of what they do and your role with each firm based upon industry use values. As an example:

You are still working for a security company and after meeting with Badda Bing Bank, you find that they have a very real need for the following items:

- Stopping ATM robberies

- Monitoring the ingress/egress of employees and customers

- Forensic accounting (tracking diverted/stolen money)

- Protection of critical infrastructure (data centers, vaults, etc.)

Before meeting with others, shouldn't you consider how these needs of Badda Bing Bank might be of concern to others on the list (Fidelity To Us Corp., MyBank Inc., and Sound Money Savings Bank)?

In the course of meeting with these firms, you find that some have overlapping concerns while others have some or most of these aspects covered. However, in the discussions, your correct usage of industry jargon, understanding of banking rules and regulations and grasp of real-world knowledge of the dynamics of the banking world will help to impress (or at the very least, credentialed) you and your company as fairly knowledgeable and savvy security folks as it pertains to banking.

The knowledge base builds with each new engagement. Even working with similar industries such as banking and gaming (casino) operators informs you of the next questions, steps, or types of thinking and realities that your potential clients use or are confronted with.

Sooner than later, people in like industries will realize that you have built an expertise in their business and they are much more likely to give you their time and/or business due to this solid base of knowledge. This is how you establish core accounts that are truly strategic in your overall model for success.

The Role of WIP (Work-in-Progress) Accounts

Work-In-Progress accounts are accounts which are not necessarily strategic in nature (although they can fall into the strategic industry buckets that were aforementioned) but are the "bread and butter" accounts that give every account manager a type of regular, annuity-type work that helps to keep the lights on. These accounts should be looked into as to possible inroads into other divisions or business units to develop further.

WIP accounts are very good for various reasons such as references, referrals, and guidance in their industries. All attempts should be made to develop Internal Client Champions and getting as "sticky" as possible within these companies (see later sections).

The Role of Industry Groups and/or Associations

It is best to use core and WIP accounts' contacts to ascertain what are the industry groups or associations that have the muscle to gather, inform, and influence the members of each industry. Within each industry there may be several groups with memberships that purport to represent the industry. Also, there are strata groups that represent different levels of certifications, management, or expertise. These groups may seem daunting in stature and in their unstated purpose – to keep all others out and to work amongst themselves. But these groups are vital for your success.

This is leveraging at its finest – leveraging existing relationships. The key to groups, associations, clubs, etc. is <u>in</u> their exclusivity. These groups make it a point to exclude others from themselves for the purposes of creating distinctions, whether they be for furtherance of education, alignment of goals, improvement of industry standards, etc.

This insularity is maddening to a lot of outsiders and it should be because the point is to exclude people like you and me who want to do business with them. However, a defensive and exclusionary practice that keeps others out will work to your favor if you do one thing well – infiltrate the group through one of its members, preferably the president, executive director or main power broker.

These associations (especially the very powerful ones) create an interdependence amongst its members which makes the bonds ever tighter and the associative power ever stronger. The irony is that if you get through to one member (once again, preferably a powerful member), then you are able to leverage that associate member's guidance and referrals to other members. How does one accomplish such a feat?

Consider the purpose of these groupings. What are they there for? It does not matter whether the groups are formed as a result of: creed, profession, certification, education, training or any other selective process. They are there to bring value to their constituents. As a result of this overriding charter, the associations usually crave two things – relevance to their constituents (thereby justifying their existence) and getting something for practically nothing. That is where you come in.

Providing a service that will give more relevance or meaning for the association is one entry point. An unusually effective tool is that of providing subject matter experts (SMEs) to talk about something relevant and dear to the association. Whether it is an explanation or practical handling of new legislation that may affect the associative body or an expert on a new development (invention, iteration, or development), this type of speaking engagement is very powerful for your purposes.

The speaking engagement is actually quite inexpensive especially if you are able to parlay a speaking slot at an upcoming association get together such as a conference, convention or symposium. Speakers may or may not get remuneration but usually, if you pay for transportation, housing and meals, it is well within most sales department's budgets.

The power of this type of entry point is powerful in many ways. Firstly, an association will not feel like it is a "sell" job that you are doing in talking about your company or its products but rather it will acknowledge that it was done to "tell not sell" to its members. Secondly, the "halo" effect of a credible and respected speaker talking about something very relevant to their business such as a clinical psychologist (who is talking about workplace violence prevention) speaking to human resource management is very impactful and cogent (I should know, I've hosted many such meetings) in giving the host (that being you) major credentialing in the eyes of those attending. Credibility like that comes not from blowing one's own horn but in co-opting the power of reference (referent power in psychological terms). Should the speaker allude to services that you or your company can render, then all the better!

The next entry point in the two-pronged approach to these associations is free or practically free help. How you can do that is to offer the services of yourself or your firm in the role of an associate member or facilitator to the association you are wooing. It could be participating or donating in fundraisers, being part of a committee doing things that most people dread to do (subscription drives or fundraising) or being the resident subject matter expert in your field to them for gratis (or severely discounted rates). NOTE: this discounting would be on a limited basis in terms of engagement to the association's needs and not the individual members. The key is not to create an image in the mind of the members that you will do work for them at near poverty levels.

This is an incredibly powerful tool because it does two things simultaneously. It gives opportunity based on proximity. When you are working with very jaded people suspect of "free" help and you do this on a regular basis without self-aggrandizement, then you truly come across as someone who has the association's interest (and presumptively its members) at heart. If you are working on a subcommittee or board and have unprecedented face time, then (unless you really have the personality of Attila the Hun) it will bode well for empathy and commonalities to be discovered.

The other message that is sent is that you are there to work hard and help the association. You will not be part of the hoard trying to break into their world and being focused on transactional successes.

Now, you may think that this takes a lot of time and to a certain degree it does. However, the penetration and advancement that you will make in getting to key decision makers is truly unrivaled. This is critical. It is important to distance yourself from the competition in ways that go beyond product, service offerings, KPIs, SLAs and other defensive sieves that are put up so as to keep the masses at bay.

The irony of exclusionary trade groups and industry associations is that in getting "in" with one member allows entry to other members. This employs "word of mouth" which is very powerful indeed. So what was initially a device to keep you out is now being co-opted to give you an entrée to a body of people that you have time to personally bond with. This type of branding is priceless because you become an "insider".

In summary, the power of multiples makes the task of meeting, knowing and engaging with potential clients so much easier than just trying to get in by your own means. It is efficacious and efficient.

Chapter 13:
Aim and Shoot High

Question: How does one find the "right" decision maker within a new client prospect? And, more relevantly, how does one find that decision maker in a mammoth, global organization with tens of thousands (maybe hundreds of thousands) of employees?

People who endeavor to meet with decision makers that will consider them and their companies usually do certain things that have proven to be ineffective. Here are some common pitfalls.

1. Using software or algorithms to identify the "right" person. One of the ways is to use technology tools such as Linked In, Google, the company's website, etc. to find this elusive decision making person. These tools are extremely effective on many levels in getting information; however, the real world of multi levels of matrixed power and actual power bases not evidenced in organizational charts muddies up the search for the correct decision maker(s).

   In every organization, the titles and the locations of people does not necessarily have a direct link with the decision-making ability. This has been proven time and time again in my dealings with people I thought were decision makers hierarchically but in the end were not.

2. Networking with industry professionals that they are trying to get penetration. Another way is to rely on warm leads, tangential relationships, and friends of friends networking which invariably produces mediocre or poor results because the decision maker is seldom able to be reached through this methodology. Why is that? Think about it for a second. What are the odds (statistically) that you are going to be able to meet the one or two decision makers on project X for Goliath Incorporated (assuming that you know that such a project existed) from a series of tangential introductions?

   You would first need a clear road map as to how the relationships that start with you would end up with the key people, which would be mapped out as to show who to ask for and what to ask for. Then you would also need to know the ins and outs of how to navigate to get to those people so as to solicit them for time to speak. Even if you were to identify whom it is that you needed to ultimately talk to, you have to convince them that you are worthy to have a meeting with them. I think you can see that this is tough to do.

3. Referrals from "safe" connectors (individuals who know a lot of people) to get you an introduction to the decision maker. This is also very dicey because the people in the targeted organization that your connector knows may not be at the right level or position to help. Unless the connector that you are working with is very powerful and/or respected, most referrals fall flat. The reason is because, no matter how glowing the referral, would I (being the person asked to give the introduction to the ultimate decision maker in the targeted organization) jeopardize my job, prestige or standing in the company by connecting you to a person several rungs higher up in my organization's ladder so as to make my friend Mr. Connector happy? Not likely. I don't know you. And more importantly, I don't know what you will do in front of my boss's boss so why would I take that chance? A "no" would seem more appropriate than a "yes".

These are the more common techniques in getting to a decision maker when you are going into a situation "cold" and not knowing any way to do so. The fact is that most people shoot too low when they do try to engage with a new, potential client. Or they get lost in the vastness of the organization that they are trying to infiltrate.

So we are left with the question: how do you get to the right decision maker when confronted with a large or global entity with so many people and locales? Consider the illustration on the following page.

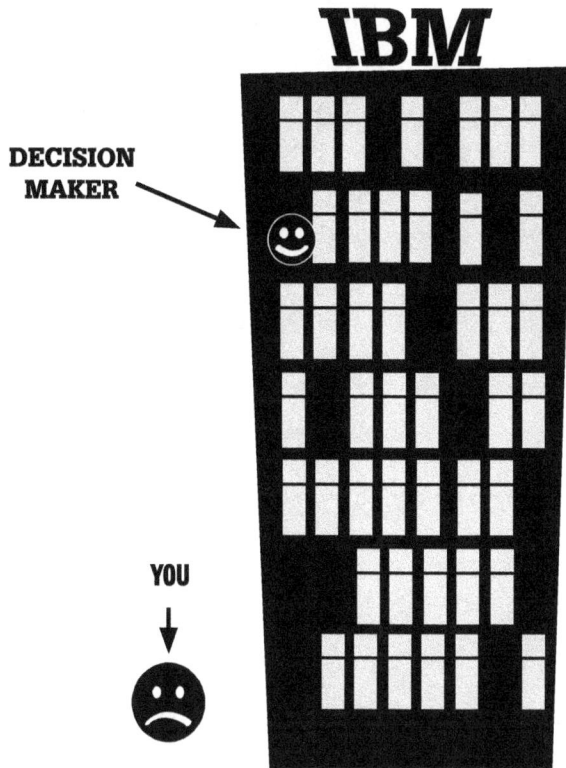

IBM

DECISION MAKER →

YOU ↓

NOTE: International Business Machines Corporation (IBM) is used as strictly for illustrative purposes. IBM's employee and contractor population are in the tens of thousands spread throughout the world and have various reporting structures (direct versus indirect)

In looking at the problem, it seems daunting indeed but it need not be. There is another approach that may seem daunting at first but is actually a way that really makes it very efficient and effective to get to the right decision maker.

I borrowed this method from Anthony Parinello's "Selling to VITO" (Very Important Top Officer) and have morphed it for my own purposes.[19] The technique is to call the CEO (or highest officer such as President) of the targeted organization. Yes, you read correctly – call the CEO or more accurately the CEO's office!

What most don't know is how powerful (and relatively easy) it is to get to the top of an organization and get to where you need to go when you are at a higher altitude.

Let's cover why you should do this and the underlying principle behind this action before we get into the mechanics of such a move. The reason is that once you get to the CEO's level, you will probably NOT talk to the CEO directly and that is totally fine. Who you really want to talk to is the CEO's administrative assistant (secretary) who is the ultimate gatekeeper. But here's the interesting thing about this particular gatekeeper. She/he keeps the gate for her/his boss (the CEO) but not for the other officers of the company such as the other C-band levels (CFO, COO, CIO, etc.,) or the vice presidents, whomever they may be.

In fact, it has been my experience that they are particularly effective in doing two things:

- Directing me to the next band down from the CEO as to the name and level (even their contact information)

- Giving me the ability to invoke her/his name to open up receptivity on the part of the next rung down

The question is begged: why would this person do this? Well, following human dynamics, most people usually fall into the camp of helpfulness as long as there is no negative repercussions for them to help you. The CEO's administrative assistant is immune from a lot of negative repercussions within the organization as this person is the CEO's right hand when it comes to agenda setting, organizing his/her calendar and impeding or allowing people to approach the throne.

As long as you are asking for guidance to talk to someone lower than her/his boss, the information is usually forthcoming. However, to get an audience with the CEO is another story. But we don't want to talk to the CEO in this case. Because, as powerful as the CEO may be within the organization, he/she is really not the appropriate person to ask for guidance on the decision maker for buying jet plane parts, security systems, building contracting, etc. The appropriate division or functional silo head is the right person to approach. While I have come across some CEO administrative assistants that do not know whom to refer me to regarding my specific request to talk to the decision maker for acquisition of BLANK product or service, I have found this to be an exception.

Usually the CEO's administrative assistant knows very well the person to talk to and will give a way to contact this person (phone or email or both). Why? Because, once again, there is no negative repercussions to do so. The administrative assistant is the de facto second most powerful person in the company by mere virtue of the fact of proximity and control of the CEO's world. Would any mere VP dare to take umbrage at being routed by CEO's assistant should they do so? The answer is no.

To illustrate this system's efficacy, I present the following:

Personal Case Citing: Act of Desperation = Inspiration

As is most of the world's source of inspiration, the genesis of this way of doing things came from an act of desperation. You see, I moved from Seattle to the Washington, D.C. area with my wife and young son with no job, no prospects, no connections (viable ones that is) and wanted to do something totally different (another industry).

I had a nine-month burn rate on my funds (that is to say, I had nine months of funds until I would be looking at living under a bridge eating pork and beans or worse). Having gone to all the following places for job searching, I became very despondent:

- Classified (want) ads of major newspapers
- Jobs online (Monster.com, Careerbuilder.com)
- Recruiting firms (head hunters)
- Networking functions (in various industries)
- Job and trade fairs
- Friends and families' connections

Does this sound familiar from your personal experience? Can you feel the level of despair that I was experiencing? So after spending five months trying these traditional routes, I started feeling a cold sweat panic start to descend upon me as I came to the realization that all these traditional or "safe" methods were going nowhere FAST!

One thought (a challenge actually) came to me – if I purport to be a masterful sales person, then what claim do I have to that appellation if I could not sell myself (the one true product that I could legitimately claim to be the most knowledgeable about – for good and for bad)? That challenge, coupled with the fact that I had four more months to left until I hit the "wall", prompted me to re-think the way of approaching the marketplace when looking for a job.

So, instead of sending out hundreds of resumes blindly so as to increase my "exposure" to the employers out there, what I did was concentrate on 15 employers, that's it. I wanted to get into the security world (something that I had no previous experience in whatsoever). I happened to read about a project called Operation Safe Commerce (OSC) funded by the Department of Homeland Security which had some of largest security-based companies in the world participating.

I co-opted that list as the main backbone of my target list. I then started to learn about OSC which was an initiative to secure ocean containers coming into the United States post 9/11. This was an interesting crossover because I did have an extensive background in logistics, especially ocean container movement which was the man emphasis of the OSC program.

In compiling the list of targeted 15 companies, I separated these companies into top 5, mid 5 and bottom 5. The companies represented were Boeing, Raytheon, SAIC, Lockheed Martin, Pinkerton Consulting and Investigations, Unisys, CH2M Hill, etc. I then researched the top 5 of the list (the companies that I thought were the most promising for whatever reason I thought at the time).

First, I researched the overall company and then drilled down on the leadership. While I was doing that, I also researched the concept behind RFID (radio frequency identification) tagging which was a very large component of OSC. I wrote a white paper from the research that I gathered.

After a point in the researching, I made a cold call script and then I called Boeing main line and asked for then CEO Phil Condit. I don't mind telling you that I was sweating! But miraculously I was patched through to Mr. Condit's assistant. I was stunned! And when I was asked what the nature of the call was, I stuttered out the fact that I wanted to talk to the person who was in charge of supply chain security within the company. This very helpful assistant gave me the name and number of the executive vice president of that division. I then thanked her and hung up. I then called the named executive vice president armed with Mr. Condit's assistant's name and I invoked it by truthfully saying that I was referred to him by her.

I did not know if this gambit would work until I got a call from that executive vice president a few hours later! When asked the meaning or purpose of the call, I told him I wanted to know if he could point me to the ACTIONABLE person within his division with whom I could talk about possibilities to do work either on a fulltime basis or contract. To my furthering amazement, he gave me his director's name and phone number! I thanked him and hung up.

I had two competing emotions at this time. One was relief due to the nervousness that was pent up. The other was elation because I thought I had found the way to effectively and decisively punch through the wall of "no's" that I had encountered.

I then proceeded to knock down the other four targeted companies using this method and sure enough they all played out accordingly! I then went through the whole list of companies (15 altogether).

The results were that I engaged with 8 firms of the tightly targeted list in multiple interviews and meetings. I was also armed with a white paper that was used instead of the ubiquitous resume. Why? Because resumes are invariably dusted with half-truths, exaggerations, and out and out lies. They also don't allow the hiring manager to see what you have to offer in terms of original ideas, ability to convey those ideas well, and level of care and preparedness that is entailed in a well-constructed idea set piece.

The outcome is that I had two job offers and I took the best of the two which did many things all at once:

1. I transitioned into a job that was in supply chain security (new industry).

2. I got a 20% increase in pay from my previous West Coast jobs (which helped immensely as DC was a lot more expensive than Seattle).

3. I got an affirmation of a system that has proven itself time and time again throughout my personal and business life. (In fact, I incorporate this into my trainings for my company right now.)

This unorthodox approach is done for many reasons. As stated before, most people shoot too low at their targets in revenue production efforts. As a result this creates very bad byproducts:

Futility and frustration. For "big ticket" items, the decision making is usually much higher up than you think. Most of the people that you encounter are constrained by budget. However, the higher you move up the food chain of the organization, the less budget considerations and their constraints play as factors. These people make the budgets and allocations, and if you have reached them, the probability is very high that you will succeed in your efforts.

The problem of appropriateness. You can have the ear of the CEO, but who is the individual that you want the action out of? Getting to that person in a monolithic company is very difficult. There is also the added layer of complexity in a decision making matrix that involves several people to ratify a decision. Going to the CEO's office gives you the 10,000 foot view of the internal structure (reporting and power) and allows engagement at those levels fairly quickly.

The issues encountered in a bid or procurement-driven process. When you engage too lowly then what happens is the apparatus of the company kicks into high gear. Procurement or sourcing is consulted and then the inevitable old saw of RFP is pulled out to put you through the rigors of "a fair bid". Well, that's all fine and well but I am not interested in being fair. I am remunerated by winning (ethically and legally) but the procurement sieve puts me into "the pack" which is definitely where I do not want to be! I am aiming for a non-bid format that will never be opened up to anyone because the decision maker really wants (and will get) what he/she wants. If, however, due to company policy the field MUST be opened to others via an RFP, then I want to have exposure to the decision maker already. The idea is so that the decision maker will help "guide" the procurement process to an eventual winner – me.

PROPOSITIONS:

1. Engage low (where most people dwell) and you will get poor or terrible results.
2. Engage at the highest ACTIONABLE level may not guarantee that you will always win work but it will increase your potential of winning dramatically.

Chapter 14:
Developing the Client Champion

There is a unique person within any company that you are targeting who is absolutely indispensable in getting into an account and maintaining growth and positive exposure within that firm. If you are fortunate enough to see the telltale signs of who this person is and to further develop a good relationship with him or her, then you will be able to go very far and deep in the targeted company in a relatively short time.

That person is called the Client Champion. This person (or persons) is the guide for you through the labyrinth of the client company. Finding, befriending, and working with this person is pivotal to the success that you may enjoy with the company that you are targeting to do business.

This Client Champion can help immeasurably by showing you the internal landscape of their company and its vested parties. The power of the Client Champion is that, with his/her support, you will be able to:

- More easily encourage the client's associates to adopt and support you and your company

- Be directed in what to do, what not to do, and areas to proceed with (or avoid) in mapping out the internal political landscape of the client company

- Be informed of opportunities that you may not have had any access to as an outsider

Furthermore, without these **Client Champions** you will find it very hard to have anyone adopt or agree to what you are proposing.

Developing Client Champions

Identifying potential **Client Champions** is the first step. But what do they look like? Is there a certain title or trait that would indicate that a person within a company is a Client Champion? Of course not! These people inhabit any position or location and have no odd attribute that would make them stand out.

However, there are telltale signs in their behavior that would give clear indications that they are the coveted Client Champions that you should pursue. Such as:

1. Head nods and smiles. When you have the initial meetings with the targeted company, take a look at the people in the room. When doing a presentation, who's asking the questions? Do they seem interested and/or sympathetic to your idea? Head nodding, smiles, and probing questions shows a certain level of interest. That is a good place to start.

2. Engage actively. It would be smart to actively engage these possible candidates for Client Champions positions. When you ask them questions regarding their company or their needs, do you get monosyllabic answers or are they genuinely giving robust good answers? Do they give you a sense that they are interested in working with you? At this stage, the people that you engage may or may not be decision makers but they certainly could be great influencers.

3. Delve into the possible motivations of the potential Client Champion involved with what you have to provide as a service or product. The more they have to benefit due to ease of service that you provide, or something that is as simple as the fact that they just like you, is a good thing.

Now that you have an idea as to who may be Client Champions, the next step is have them help you! Ask them for help in what is the best way to engage with the company. Go from a very fundamental, almost philosophical way of approaching the target company to more specificity. This is invaluable because it teaches you how the company's mindset works.

Every company has its own culture. Sometimes even divisions within a company have their own culture. In asking the Client Champion on how to approach the company or group, you are doing two things.

First, you are getting valuable information as to how to approach the company in tone, pace and technique. A firm that does not like pushy salespeople will not accept that kind of approach no matter how "persuasive" you may think you are with that approach. A division that values giving a new vending partner a shot, but not at the detriment of their current vending partners, will not give you a lot of business right at the start. But you'll know that they will be just as loyal to you should you win more of their business.

Second, you are sending the message to the Client Champion that you are worthy of support because you listen and you act accordingly. This is important because it makes it more palatable to support someone that you like and that also listens!

How can the Client Champion help?

Insight. That's how the Client Champion can help. He/she can peel back the veil of the company to reveal the following things:

1. Formal structures. While it may seem very simple in looking at an organization chart to determine how divisions or groups are organized, the fact remains that a lot of the organization charts are not available to outsiders (even of public companies). Another impediment is that, as with most human endeavors, the documentation is not always in synch with the real power structures within a company.

2. Informal structures. As aforementioned, the real power structures within a firm are hardly ever delineated in an organization chart. Just because a person is the head of a department or division does not necessarily mean that they are the final or only decision maker for that entity. The Client Champion can help to flesh out where the real power lies and how to co-opt those power people to your cause.

3. Company likes/dislikes. Companies, like people, have things that they really, really like and things that they abhor. If the Client Champion states that you should never do any PowerPoints at meetings, then guess what? Don't do them! If the Client Champion says that the company's managers love vending partners who work with them as a team and keep everyone notified and involved, then guess what? Do that. It may seem very simplistic because it is. The results you from adapting these traits will get you far!

4. Company agendas. There are many divergent agendas housed in the

four walls of a company which are invariably driven by person or persons of influence or power. Client Champions may not be those people of power but, if they help you to know what these agendas are (even if the agendas are against your company), then they are rendering a great service to you. They may even help you get the sale of a lifetime (see the next Personal Case Citing).

It is important for you to ask how to build your case internally and lobby (with Client Champion's help) the people that would approve a project or initiative.

Personal Case Citing: The Nail That Stuck Out

When I worked for an ocean container line company, I had a very boisterous boss who was wont to do impetuous things like spitting in the wind. Let me be more specific.

We had a customer called Monolith Inc. that was a HUGE exporter of freight but not when it came to our share. My boss, Derek, was very upset that our competition was getting thousands of containers a year but we were limping along with 500 containers a year globally (which was .05% of their annual freight volumes) and that was it! I was also very frustrated but I just got this account and didn't know all the players.

Derek said he would approach Monolith Inc. with a pricing schedule that would actually lower the shipping rates but they had to give us more business based on set volume thresholds to receive this pricing. He would make it clear that we were tired of doing the small stuff and that we demand to have more volume.

As we drove to Monolith Inc.'s headquarters, I told Derek that, even though I applauded his bravado, I thought that his approach was not going to be received well. Derek told me to just do the PowerPoint presentation and leave the pricing discussion to him. I shrugged with resignation of the fact that I could not dissuade him of this tact.

When we met with the key players of Monolith's shipping department (all seven of them) headed by Thomas C., I had a sinking feeling in my stomach. I did the presentation as planned and about a third of the way into the presentation, I was interrupted by Derek who couldn't wait anymore to spring the announcement to Monolith Inc. Derek said "Listen, we need to talk about rates and volumes. We are willing to lower our rates but you need to give us a whole lot more volume than what we are getting. It's just that simple!"

Judy, one of Thomas C.'s managers and who had a reputation for being very tough, looked at Thomas C. as if asking for permission. Thomas nodded his head. Judy, staring icily at Derek, then said: "Derek, in your statement I heard an ultimatum." Derek stammered "Know, I-I-I just thought that for our pricing we should get reciprocity!" Judy continued, "Oh no, I don't think it was anything other than an ultimatum. And here at Monolith we never take that well. Do you understand?" Derek said sheepishly, "Yes."

With the very awkward moment that just occurred, I didn't know what to do except to go on doing the presentation. So that is what I did. As I proceeded ahead everyone started to become less tense, I noticed someone who just didn't fit in (James). You see, Monolith Inc. was a very conservative company in every sense of the word. They were conservative in thinking, in behavior and in dress and grooming. Suit and tie and short hair were de rigueur. But James was unlike anyone at Monolith or even in most companies.

James was 60ish at the time with flowing white long hair that was in a ponytail and extended past his shoulders. He wore a clean white shirt with a bolo tie. He also had a long beard that was more salt than pepper. He kind of looked like the photographer Ansel Adams only in a corporate setting.

He stuck out from all the rest of the corporate squares like a sore thumb! He also was the only person who was nodding and writing copious notes from my presentation. I made a point of getting his business card.

Later on that day, I thought I'd take a chance on a hunch! I called James. This is what transpired:

John: "I wanted to call and apologize to you for our performance today."

James: "This was not your fault. However, you do need to tell your boss to tone it down and NEVER do what he did if you ever want business from us."

John: "I read you loud and clear and will convey that to Derek. Could I ask you a question on another matter?"

James: "Shoot."

John: "How do I get your company's business in a big way?"

James: "John, you have to be patient but above all you have to make it easy to be used."

John: "What do you mean by that?"

James: "What I mean is that when I make a container booking (reserving a container and the space on a vessel), you should make it so easy that all I have to do is to tell you how many units I have to ship and from where to where and what the timeframe is."

John: "How do I do that?"

James: "Create a cell unit that is totally dedicated and knowledgeable about Monolith and we'll give you a try. A cell unit made up of customer service, operations, equipment, etc."

Upon that advice, I went back and worked on getting a team together so that we could truly do that. It wasn't hard but the initial efforts were a bit awkward due to our lack of knowledge of all the specifications of Monolith. But James was a man of his word because he gave us more freight. First it was in dribs and drabs but then, as we became better at the task, we got more and more business. Pretty soon others from the shipping department were giving us a chance upon James' recommendations and using us for their tradelanes.

I was speechless at the ease by which we got so much business. James was a font of knowledge as to who liked what and what did or did not work with their company. He was a sounding board for me when I bounced off new ideas on how to grow or get business from Monolith. There were times that James said that if I just waited for a few months, then a new piece of business would open up and it surely came to pass. James also was blunt in saying when we would never get the business away from the existing competition because they were too embedded into the tradelane.

The result is that, instead of 500 containers per year volume, I raised our volume with Monolith to 5,000+ containers per year! This was done solely through the help of James, an incredible man that became a friend in the process of doing business because he cared enough to give a newbie a break!

5. Notice of new projects that you would not have knowledge of or visibility. Client Champions are able to give you insight into people or things that you never would have known if it were not for their help. They signal to you impending projects or changes. This could be for expansion of business or protection of your position with the client company.

One example of this came when I was on a social/business call with Alfonso, a good friend and business colleague with a very large manufacturing company.

He was the head of security for a very large Fortune 100 company. In my position as the head of security consulting sales and marketing, I landed their business for security consulting and investigations on a master service contract basis. Months later, I was chatting when all of a sudden he said to me "John, would you like a chance to compete for a very large global contract for all our background investigations?" I blinked and thought he was kidding me or at least just taunting me. He smiled as I said "yes".

Alfonso then gave me the name of his colleague in the company who was about to float out an RFP for his business. After quite an amount of work, we won that one as well! In looking back at the dynamics of what transpired, had Alfonso not told me of the work in advance, I would not have had any particular advantage to win.

How to Take Care of Your Client Champion

Let me take a breather and explain the modus operandi behind Client Champions. A Client Champion is not just a vehicle for your success. He or she is an equal partner with you on your success and his/her success. There is no remuneration from you (illegal and unethical) and there is no collusion to fix prices or markets or anything that smacks of that. The idea of Client Champion is one of collaboration in the finest sense of the word.

The Client Champion, if he or she is truly a friend, will also watch your back. Therefore, you should do all that is within your power to help protect them and not have them hurt or compromised as a result of doing business with you. There are some things that you can do to maintain this unique relationship.

DO NOT put the Client Champion in an awkward position because of their support for you. This involves appearances such as inappropriate gifts or considerations. Keep it all within legal guidelines of your company and that of his/her company. Keeping confidentiality of information that they share with you is key critical. If you find that you cannot keep confidentiality, then this arrangement will not last long. Don't even think of asking for information that would seriously put them in harm's way. If they volunteer such information, then be very, very careful as to how you use it. Short-term gains are not worth killing a great relationship.

DO NOT ask Client Champions to defend you at the cost of their own position. Sometimes the Client Champion's company will not support you or your company even with the protestations of internal staff. It is then you must realize not to take it "personally" even though the first inclination is to do so. To emotionally strong arm someone to back you up will not only end in failure, but may sever (or needlessly strain) the cords of the relationship. No Pyrrhic victory is worth it.

DO protect the Client Champion whenever feasible and ethical to do so. Reciprocity is key to any relationship. If you are called to defend or protect the Client Champion, do so within ethical and legal bounds. Sometimes it is important to have distance so that there is no appearance or actuality of rampant favoritism.

Proposition: In the vetting of potential Client Champions, it is best to consider some categories of people within the client organization that may help (or may not help) your cause:

Influencers – These are people that may or may not have decision-making powers but they definitely have the ability to influence others within their orbit of influence in the organization.

Decision Makers – These are people that have the power to make a definitive decision and back it up with action. They have the mandate to make decisions, the budgets to finance the decisions and the political willpower to fund/finance the decisions. They may be an individual or a group. In order to be a decision maker, you have to pass two thresholds of definition:

1. You have the authority over a budget - to fund a project or initiative

2. You have the ability (political will) to spend the budgeted funds

Doers – These are people who carry out the work or functions but are not empowered to make decisions nor do they have control of budgets. They do have some influence but generally fall into the Vetoers category (see below).

Vetoers – These are individuals who have the power to say "no" or block an initiative but no <u>real</u> power to act or say a definitive "yes" to anything whether it be projects, budgets or initiatives. They tend to be defenders of the status quo.

Posers – These are individuals that may project the image that they are decision makers but ultimately they are not. They may even be in key roles or titles (e.g., director or vice president) but they do not have the requisite power to enact anything. (See definition of Decision Makers)

In working with the myriad of people that populate any organization, you have to do a bit of profiling as to their position, behavior and probability in helping you through the process of getting business from them. Once again, if you do a little homework upfront, it will save you a ton of work on the back end.

Chapter 15:
Getting Sticky With It

In approaching a potential client, one must plan the point of entry and the ability to move up, down, left, right and diagonally in the organization from that point of entry. The operative plan is to get in at the right level (see Chapter 13) and then to move forward in different directions with the help of the Client Champion (see Chapter 14) so as to maximize your level of entrenchment. The purpose is to be as nearly indispensable as possible. We all know that no one that is indispensable to any organization; however, the task at hand is to be as nearly indispensable as possible.

Point of Entry Planning

One must plan the approach of an account with altitude in mind: the higher the initial point of contact, the better, as we have illustrated in Chapter 13. It is also just as important to look at the area that you enter into a company or the point of entry. If everyone in your industry goes after the same department as you are, then what do you think your results would be? Is it easier to go down a well-trodden path? The answer would be yes. However, doing that which is easy and expedient usually yields the least returns. The fields that everyone works in usually are gleaned of all the fruits.

However, if you look to a different field to work in, then, while it may be unorthodox, it may lead to greater returns because not a lot of folks (if any) have tilled that field.

> *Example: when you are a security provider, the natural person to call on is the security chief of a company. That would be the natural progression of things. However, when you call on that person, you will probably find a couple of things happening.*

1. Crushing amount of vendors calling on this person – this comes from the fact that everyone in security is beating a path to talk to the security director. In certain writings, it is called vendor fatigue. With this level of overwhelming amount of people trying to get on that director's docket,

it would naturally cause vendor fatigue. It is hard not to be "jaded" in light of this setup.

2. Answers to problems have already been given. You may think you have the true answer; however, there are probably a lot of solutions already in place. There are also relationships that are already cemented. This combination may be hard to beat.

3. The security director is looking at you using the security "lens" and nothing else. This is a very commonly overlooked problem. In our example, the security director will think and look at things with one set of thinking that is derived from his experiences (such as law enforcement, as an example), which is totally normal. However, is that really who you want to call on? You see, with that type of thinking comes the limitation of looking at your product or service from a security director or former law enforcement perspective. He will not look at your product/service as a person from HR or finance or IT or some other discipline or background.

This limitation of the security director in perceiving the uses of your product/service could have a severely negative impact for you and your company. Security directors usually think along security lines because that is what their experiences have informed them to do.

This may kill a project due to no perceived need for your product or service. However, someone from legal counsel may see things a little differently. They may see the legal downside of not using your product or service as foolish due to liability issues.

Calling on others with varied backgrounds and disciplines may open up your product/service to a myriad of applications heretofore not thought of, which also opens up areas of revenue that you may never have known had you only talked to the beleaguered security director! (See case citing below on a product that iterated itself to suit the needs of different users (and uses) than for which it was originally intended.)

4. Control freak behavior or territorialism may set in with the security director. This, unfortunately, is a very common malady that people who are insecure succumb to. The problem is that once you call on the

security director, he may give you a trickle of business or no business but then he expects you to ONLY deal with him and no one else. This is a very bad quandary because, while you are not getting any sales traction with this guy, you also can't go to anyone else because he has made himself your only entrée to his company. If he finds out that you have circumvented him, he may potentially cut you off.

Case Citing – Products that changed based on use

Remember Arm and Hammer Baking Soda? If you don't, your mother and grandmother sure does! It is a major ingredient in their baking repertoire because it is one of those ingredients that you always need when baking cakes, breads, etc.

But baking skills, as with a lot of homemaking, have gone severely by the wayside because of our changing lifestyles. Home baking is a dying art form.

So what do you do if your product is fast becoming obsolete? Well, you look at what your product can do beyond its most popular application.

Consequently, you have Arm and Hammer Baking Soda refrigerator and freezer deodorizer, toothpaste, shoe freshener, amongst the various iterations that you can take the initial product into.

Employing the Stickiness Factor

How then do you engage with the client when you gain entry into the firm through previously untapped channels? You start with proposing or doing the work in one department and then by leveraging a Client Champion then you get them to help to evangelize you, your company and what wonderful things you can do for them (See Chapter 14: Developing the Client Champion).

As in the case of the personal citing of Chapter 14, my personal Client Champion was actively extolling the virtues of what we did for him to his colleagues and that had an incredible multiplier effect on our business.

The key is to get sticky with the client and push the boundaries whenever appropriateness and opportunity may allow. However, there will be times when you will be told not to proceed into certain areas or go down certain paths. Heed that advice well and don't try to win them over with your charm because your Client Champion will know the ropes a whole lot better than you ever will.

If invited to go (or allowed to go) somewhere to do some exploratory work, then do so. Have cursory conversations with various departments, functions, locations, and levels. The purpose is to spread out and increase your "touch point" contacts until you have a fairly good coverage of the company's personnel and their true hierarchical structures. Knowledge of the company's ins and outs is crucial to avoid land mines that you may stumble across if not advised in advance. It is usually the things that "you don't know that you don't know" that may hurt you in the end.

The migration policy has a dual use in that it may help you to identify possible opportunities and usages for your product or services in ways that only the client personnel could envisage due to the intimacy of their knowledge of their own company.

Help Clients Navigate Through Their Own Systems

When working with monolithic firms, their gigantic size and complexity can work against them. There are ways in which you can materially affect positive change within your client's world. Here are some ways that may significantly increase your positive exposure with your client by having them come to you for ways to deal with their sheer size.

1. Requests For Proposals (RFP). When I am invited to participate in RFPs to work on (of the ones that I rarely accept), my goal is to endeavor to help the client get an accurate and helpful response in spite of the fact that most RFPs are atrociously written. **Many client company's vested parties have confessed to me that they cannot stand their own vetting processes due to overly complex RFPs and lack of clarity.**

2. Guidance. If you help your clients from the beginning to fixate clearly on what the issue at hand may be and how you would address them,

it would bode well with you. No matter how big or small a company and even if they are very prideful, truly helpful assistance or guidance is appreciated. Too often your competition will not mention a problem (and how to solve it) because they are afraid that they would appear to be too critical of the client. Sometimes vending partners treat EVERYTHING as a billable event and, while I am not suggesting you do pro bono work on a regular basis, it is also helpful to provide some guidance where it is done as part of relationship building and not always attached to a fee!

3. Matchmaking. Another helpful tactic is to bring operational folks from your company into the equation very quickly so as to increase stickiness not only with you but on a peer-to-peer level. This has been very crucial in helping to cement the relations between two companies because the client company's folks can see and vet your people and decide very quickly that you are a worthy partner.

4. Create a better paradigm. Link or streamline services to multiple parties in what you have to offer. This is a real problem with a lot of clients which is visibility and coordination. If you can offer a "dashboard" capability or a unifying report to give your client company better information about their world, then it really will separate you from the rest of the pack in a very positive fashion. It is key, however, to offer something of real substantive value and not just contrived window dressing.

5. Offer services that come from very specific and internally driven specifications

    a. Determine if an embedded employee is a good option for you and your services. There are some cases that this makes a lot of sense. Talk about being enmeshed with a client! But it really has to make sense operationally and financially.

    b. Morphed services. Sometimes you may start on a program or plan and it simply changes due to outside conditions or the client's needs have changed. If that is the case, then be flexible enough to change to make sure that there is not a knee-jerk reaction to saying "NO" which tends to be the operative answer from most operational entities.

c. Dedicated services. Are there things that you can do for your client on a dedicated basis? Perhaps a cell unit or task force solely dedicated to the needs of the client? This may be quite an investment on the part of your company but the level of service, familiarity (on both sides) and cooperative élan could be phenomenal! This kind of setup is extremely hard to break, either by the client or a rival firm, because, if it runs well (and I have seen this work very well), then it takes on a life of its own.

d. Take on whole functions (or major parts of them). Very large firms are outsourcing so much of their infrastructure. Once sacrosanct functions such as human resource, IT, finance and even legal have been shuttled off to other companies of which some are half a world away! While this may be of concern to the internal employee population of the client company, this may work very much to the favor of vending partner companies. The smartest and swiftest can pick up on that need and capitalize very well.

With all these suggestions of what to do there are also things that you should never do:

1. Stay out of internal politics as much as possible and avoid taking sides. This really should be self-explanatory. You may get caught in the cross fire of an internal power struggle and then be left out. That may still be the case even if you don't take sides, but the odds are upped quite a bit more if you embarked on the favoritism strategy

2. Utilize the power of reliance, but don't abuse it. Be careful not to become arrogant or think that the client is so intertwined with you that they can't operate without you! This type of hubris can only bring about your own downfall. There is also a point wherein you must be careful not to be so close as to lose your own personal or corporate identity and then lose a certain needed objectivity

Personal Case Citing: The Gift That Keeps on Giving

I was working on a very large RFP with a chemical giant. We won the bid and worked it to death as far as the quality and focus that it rightly deserved. I think that, based on that initial work, my Client Champion opened up the doors to others because I was contacted by other department heads to see if I could help them. Of course, the answer was always yes. To date, we have worked on assignments for 5 divisions based on the initial strength of word-of-mouth which migrated outward.

By now you have probably gotten the hang of doing the necessary homework internally and externally to have a fairly good understanding of where you are in your business environment. Good. You'll need to have that level of confidence in tackling the next stage. Don't let the next section's name fool you; it is not a re-hashing of Chapter 7 and Chapter 8 concepts dealing with Use Value. It incorporates what we've covered in those chapters and puts real life spins on them. However, it would be good to restate some earlier propositions to remind you of the basic tenets that we stated. They are:

CHAPTER 7:
MISUNDERSTANDINGS OVER "VALUE" PROPOSITIONS:

1. The true value of something is in the <u>USE</u> the client can gain from that something (product, service, or company that provides either). In other words, use of something determines its worth (value) to the buyer or user and NOT the price of the product. Another way of saying this is: buyers (clients) have use values for the products that are in the marketplace. The higher the use values of a product, the more the client is willing to pay the price to attain it.

2. It is imperative to know your client's use value (or usages) of your product, company or of you – in order to be successful to know what their motivation for purchasing is and at what price it would be.

Stated plainly:

VALUE does not equal PRICE

VALUE is not related to PRICE

VALUE of something is equal to the USE of something

USE VALUE = the worth of the uses (hidden or otherwise) of something in the eye of the user

USE VALUE dictates PRICE

CHAPTER 8:

KNOW THY CUSTOMER PROPOSITION:

The USE of a product or service usually transcends the physical nature of the product itself. That is to say, there are many powerful and potent use values embedded in you, your company and your product/service that you may not be aware of. However, once you find them out, these are powerful tools at your disposal.

So let's see how, armed with the idea of Use Value, you can work more effectively with people in the business world!

Sub Section: UNDERSTANDING USE VALUE
(in Real Life Situations)

Chapter 16:
What is the Client Really Saying?

As we have found, the word "value" is really overused and misused but it points to something that people really want. Beyond the corporate smokescreens about what the buying company seeks in terms of value, the real thrust of what they want is the uses of your product, service or entity -- the uses that they (the ultimate buyer) will derive – personally or professionally. But seldom is that made clear in the business world. If you doubt it, then think back to how many times in your professional life that anyone said the following (or a version thereof):

"I don't care about all your bells and whistles of your product/service, I just care about looking like a superstar in picking the 'right' company to service my needs."

OR

"I am scared of making the wrong decision because that could be a career killer in my company's eyes."

I've never heard those words coming out of anyone's mouth during a vendor vetting. Nothing like that was ever stated in a Request For Proposal throughout all my 29+ years in business selling. But, really, that is what the decision maker(s) really think of when they make a decision. Every decision is fraught with possibilities of screw-ups and missteps, and that is why companies big and small devote so much time to vetting and examining from various metrics the abilities of possible vendors or suppliers. Who's screw-ups or missteps? The decision maker(s)! Not that all decisions have so much weight behind them but, as the level of impact on the buying company goes up (in terms of cost, market risk, company image and/or reputation), the decisions become more and more torturous for all concerned – not just the selling company.

So, it is important as a representative of the selling company to listen as well as hear what is truly being said. As opaque as some situations may lend themselves, due to buyer reluctance to show you their hand, you can spot "tells" in the conversations and how buyers comport themselves during these RFPs or negotiation talks. Poker players (at least the recent rash of them) wear sunglasses during high stakes poker so that the opponents do not see their eyes because the eyes are a form of "tell", that is to say, indicator of the true intention of the poker player.

In a way, you can see or perceive the "tells" the client is giving you by the things that they say or don't say. I break clients into two categories for simplicity sake – ones I want and ones I do not want.

Let's start with easy ones - the ones I do not want – now or ever!

Clients to Avoid:

1. Clients that talk about price/cost all the time. If you begin a conversation or get an inquiry from a possible client but their tilt, conversation and thrust all point toward price and how to get the lowest price, then you are on the trail of a price monger. The price monger tends to be very large because that is their model for profit, i.e., small margins made up by massive quantities. The price monger is seldom happy with the price given to him because everyone else (your competition) is throwing themselves at them and lowering the price.

    There are two reasons why I don't pursue clients like these. One, it is very difficult to win using the price trigger unless you want to slash your profitability to gain the account. Two, once the account is "attained", you will find that the price monger will come after you again and again with competitive pricing for you to lower your already-lowered pricing! The ground you stand on with the client is soft and sinking sand. There is no permanency to this relationship because everything is predicated on lowering your prices which you cannot do indefinitely.

2. Clients that want favors or "freebies". This type of potential client is looking to get the proverbial something for nothing. They lure you and others with the promise of great volumes (as the price monger above also does) but in return they want "bundling" of services that you would

normally offer pricing in an a la carte fashion but he wants it in an "all you can eat" format.

The main reason why this client is not acceptable is because, in giving away your products/services by "bundling" them, you are effectively taking money out of your own pocket and simultaneously cheapening your brand. How long will it be in the vast leaky sieve of the business world when others will find out that you have done this concession for this customer and they had to pay for the services? And would the resultant blowback in upset clients be worth the victory of this usually fickle type of client?

Personal Case Citing: The Loss Leader

One day I got a call from a fairly independent VP of operations while I was with a security consultancy. Henry seldom called for client advice so when he called to ask me how I would respond to a request by a potential large client, I was somewhat surprised.

Henry told me that a very large supplier of beef hamburger patties for a gigantic fast food chain restaurant had 11 factories in Asia that they wanted our company to do risk assessments on. Henry was told that, while there were several folks bidding for the business, the reputation of our company was as such that Andre (the buyer) would feel comfortable to give us the business for all 11 of the sites if we were to give him a sample of the type of work and quality we produce in doing one factory risk assessment for free.

This was a very big carrot dangled in front of a very hungry Henry, but he wanted to know how I would react if I were in his shoes. I said that I am glad Andre asked him instead of me because I would reach through the phone and try to strangle him! First, if he already favored our company based on our "reputation" of quality and good work, why would he then ask us to cheapen ourselves just to get his work? Second, would Andre shill for a customer who said he would like to give him their account but he had to provide one free 40-foot refrigerated container load of beef patties just to "make sure" that the quality was still intact?

Henry thought the better of it and called Andre to say that there would be no gratis work. Andre was rebuffed and not happy. Later, when I inquired of Henry of what happened to this situation, I was told that Andre actually came back and gave Henry an initial assessment at full book rate (no freebies or discounting). But that was it in terms of any more business. We feared that he took that one paid assessment and replicated it for the other ten sites, which is the height of stupidity.

3. Clients that allow no engagement except through one channel and are highly mechanical in the process of selection (electronic systems). In this age of technology and systems, I find that more and more buying companies (especially of a very large size) hide behind the twin buffers of a procurement department and a procurement management system (Ariba, Convergys, etc.) While in some circles (especially procurement circles) this may pass for best practices, I think it truly wipes out the real-life information and dialogue so necessary in making critical choices. Imagine if you conducted your life's choices that way – "please fill out this electronic form if you are interested in going out with me and, depending on the reply, I will get back to you".

The blind and/or severely limited nature of such transactions should automatically infer to you that you are not needed on an individual basis but rather you are part of the unwashed pack. Unless you like to be rejected or treated like cattle, don't get into these transactions.

As a colleague of mine, Dwayne Gulsby, once said: "We should go from being needed to being wanted." I'll explain later in the Personal Branding section.

Personal Case Citing: What's the Big Deal?

I once called on a potential client in the Midwest, Barney, who was rude and very standoffish over the phone. He was a security director for a very large fast food restaurant company (Shucky's) and he was being purposely difficult. However, due to pluck and perseverance, I got a meeting scheduled with this director. This is while I worked for a security consultancy.

I went to meet him with my operations director, Jimmy. As we got past the perfunctory introductions, and as I was about to sit down, this is what Barney said.

Barney (B): "I don't know why I consented to see you. You guys in security are all the same. You're no better and no worse than your competition."

Mind you, I hadn't fully sat down yet. It was after he said that that I stood up and stuck out my hand, which he quizzically shook.

John (J): "Barney, that's it then. We're done. Goodbye."

(B): "What? What are you doing?"

(J): "I am ending this meeting because you obviously have shown no interest or respect for who I am or what I do."

(B): "I was just kidding…"

(J): "No, you really weren't. When you say that, you demean not only my industry but also my company."

A tense moment passed with Jimmy, my operations guy, looking at both of us very intently.

(B): "Okay, good point. I am sorry that I said those things about your company. Please sit down."

(J): "Thank you"

We sat down and it was then that we began the meeting in earnest.

---

4. Clients that make you feel like you should be lucky to even be considered. There are some clients that take on this attitude that you (the seller) should feel lucky to be even in the running for their business. This type of thinking usually comes from very large clients that everyone in the industry covets to have in their business portfolio. The problem is that these very large clients acquire a superiority complex. They think that everyone should bend to their will and they tend to guise this in the form of "RFPs", "KPIs", and "SLAs" to set standards that almost always bend the transactional balance of power to them.

   Because there are so many suitors, these large firms are very nonchalant about who their suppliers and channel partners are because, for every one vendor, there are twenty others behind them.

   If you are selling to these firms, then know that the road to getting their business is fraught with challenges due to their demands and the uncertainty of whether or not you will be replaced by someone "sexier" in terms of pricing, terms, deliverables, etc. This type of unease does not engender confidence in the relationship and rightfully so because a lot of these relationships are not based on the fundamental building blocks of knowledge, understanding use value and reciprocity relationships, and exploration. Instead, these relationships take on a master/servant aspect that, to me, is quite repugnant. It's as if you were married for ten years but still had to constantly bat potential suitors away from your wife who, in this case, is more than willing to entertain them.

Personal Case Citing: The Double Standard

One of my directors was pursuing a very large and tony, high-end retailer to do protection work for their stores and some key events that they had. Todd, my director, felt he had a personal advantage in competing for this business as he was a former loss prevention director at this very prestigious national brand retailer known for their glitz factor and moneyed customers.

An RFP was issued to be completed by the competing companies. But as Todd and I were looking at the document, we noticed something that made me dubious of our success in the whole matter. The request asked for the cost of doing business with all its components and the markup to make sure that there would be, in the words of the RFP, "fairness and balance" in the margin.

This was an affront to both Todd and me as this retailer is/was famous for its very high markups. Todd personally knew of this and cited many times their fabulously thick margins. I asked Todd to call the procurement person to tell them our stance of NOT giving such information out but that in every manner we would comply with their requests. I didn't have high hopes.

When Todd called, he respectfully told Nia, the procurement person of our stance, and Nia promptly took umbrage at the idea that we would ask to be recused of providing the costing and margins. She did not understand why we would do that and wondered (out loud) why we would hide such information. Todd patiently told her that we weren't hiding anything but felt that there was no need to provide that information. When Nia confronted Todd further, Todd said that if our clients could afford our service, liked our results and the pricing was competitive with what is out in the marketplace, then why would or (and more importantly) should the retailer care?

Nia retorted that they wanted to know the cost breakdown and profit margin to avoid "excessive profits". To this, Todd started to see red. Todd asked her a question.

Todd (T): "Would you ever list the cost plus margin of the apparel you are selling to your customers in any of your stores?"

Nia (N): "Certainly not, it's none of their business."

(T): "Why is it 'none of their business'?"

(N): "If they can afford it, then they'll buy it. But if they can't, then they won't. It's as simple as that!"

(T): "Right. That, coincidentally, is the same premise under which we work! So, why is it acceptable for your company to be able to do that and not for us?"

Todd could hear that Nia was getting apoplectic. Furthermore, Todd continued, he personally knew the retailer's 50% or more profit margins. He also knew that sometimes the markups would be in a factor of multiples.

Needless to say, Nia was not too happy and was adamant in keeping to their policy stating that other companies (beyond ours) were totally willing to offer such information without any qualms. Todd said that we would not and as such pulled out of the running.

I am never happy when we walk away from potential profits but this one was easy. If this retailer was so blind as to their hypocrisy and yet was so inflexible to see that their business pricing model was the mirror image of ours (and so in turn they should truly understand), then I wanted no part in their self-delusion. Had we consented to demean ourselves that way, it would be the beginning of a trail of tears!

Clients to Embrace:

5. Clients that give you a lot of latitude to present your product. This may be perceived as a "bad" thing for very structured sellers who are not used to selling their product/service in an innovative or non-templated fashion. However, it really should not be seen as a problem or a negative but rather it should be perceived as a golden opportunity! Why? Because if the client gives you place to present, within a general format, your product or service in your own distinctive way, then it opens up huge possibilities to creating a message that you can hand tailor to your best advantage.

This type of latitude may come from poor vendor vetting on the part of the buying company or it may also be that the potential client wants to see you "out of the box" in terms of what you can do to creatively and persuasively present to them why you are the most deserving to receive their business.

When given a chance, don't shrink back from such a task but instead embrace it and let the creative juices flow!

Personal Case Citing: Giving the Client the World

A very large and global chemical company was vetting companies to find out who would be the best source for their global intellectual property protection work. They were looking at my security consultancy company and kept the RFP process fairly loose as to form and even content. I talked it over with my management team and we agreed that to take the boring old route of PowerPoint slides and verbose RFP response would be fatal for us due to the fact that others would probably do the same and we would subsequently be lost in the "blahness" of the competition.

The RFP issue was further compounded with three phases of the RFP that each, in its own right, would have been quite a lot of work in terms of depth, breadth and complexity. This RFP process took four months to complete and we threw everything into it that would make a positive impression such as facts, figures, case studies, global mapping of our capabilities, etc. But the nagging sense of generic RFP response kept hounding us. When we got to the finals stage and we were asked to present to the selection committee, we came up with a great idea. The key to this client was our abilities to do work well around the world and in various markets.

They wanted to know that whoever got the business would be an expert in those parts of the world that they were interested in (which was quite a lot of area) and that they could be guided by the vendor through the maze of intellectual property issues. So the issue was credibility and trust. We hit upon the idea of not just having our relevant world practice heads calling into the presentation to talk to this large chemical company but rather we would fly these very credible and realistic experts to the meeting in person. We felt that it was inadequate to have the usual worldwide teleconference with faceless people over the line. There was no substitute for personal interaction and face-to-face time, especially at such a crucial juncture.

We flew in our foreign colleagues at our considerable expense and inconvenience. The practice leaders represented South America, EMEA (Europe Middle East, Africa) and Asia were all gathered together for the presentation.

The presentation opened up and we let our foreign practice heads present for their sections along with an interactive dialogue of questions, comments, and answers. It was an immediate hit! The selection committee of nine people representing various departments of the global chemical company really were impressed by the fact that we flew these knowledgeable folks out to address their questions and concerns. Don't misunderstand. The chemical giant's folks did not go easy on us and in some cases were very critical and asked very detailed questions of our foreign practice heads. There were some answers that were far from perfect in terms of the fact that we did have limitations and could not do everything that the chemical giant wanted.

In spite of, or maybe because of, our realistic approach and the fact that there was so much real-life credibility that our foreign leaders had lent to the proceedings, it was announced soon thereafter that we won the worldwide bid! The gamble paid off big!

---

6. Clients that engage with you many times with many parties involved and in many ways (phone, person, teleconference, Webex). This is another clue as to the seriousness of purpose that would-be clients may telegraph to you of their intentions. Potential clients that tend to get many of their constituents involved in selecting the right candidate company and then allow dialogue of various members with your company is a sign that bodes well for your possible success. A company that really is not interested would not invest the time and energies to allow this type of open dialogue amongst many members to take place. It is only in the process of gathering information, asking questions of different facets of your world, company, and product/service that really shows the client's level of interest in you and how they view you in the role of helping them.

Personal Case Citing: The Mystery of the Persistent Potential Client

It is a rare set of circumstances that come together which is represented in this next case citing. To be more specific, I am unaccustomed to the following things happening on a potential client:

- Getting a sales lead from a trade show that actually led to something real

- Having the client show an inordinate interest in my company (for no explicable reason)

- Our company getting a clear field to win this client's business without RFPs or what not

So let me relate this story to you. I went to one of our security industry functions in California and did not expect to get anything palpable in terms of business from this event. (I've been to four different annual trade shows of our industry with absolutely nothing to show for it. Hence my aversion to these things.)

However, this one time a woman came up to the booth and introduced herself as Rhonda who was one of the mid-level managers of a worldwide consultancy and she asked if my company did pre-employment screening of people (criminal, civil litigation, education, employment checks) and due diligence of companies. I answered yes to both categories. She seemed mildly interested and said that she wanted to explore further our capabilities.

I followed up with her a few weeks later and she said that her procurement people would contact her. Uh oh. To me that is not a buy signal but the beginning of a trail of tears (usually my tears). But Janene from procurement called me and began to ask me questions about who we were and what we did. I assigned my very capable sales director to the job and, as time passed, Janene introduced other folks: Tonya of procurement and Alicia, representing the group needing the service.

As we spoke further and did more demonstrations, we kept on getting more and more operationally driven questions such as timeframes, costs, deliverables, system integration, etc. which is usually a VERY good sign. Then one day they said they wanted an MSA (master service agreement) signed. This was done without any RFI, RFQ, or RF anything. After a bit of legalese being thrown around...voila! The MSA was signed.

I neglected to tell you that there was NO pricing discussion. No gratuitous wrangling of rates, terms or conditions. It went eerily very smoothly as if they really didn't care what the rate was (as long as it was "reasonable").

At the time of this writing I still am thinking through why we were so fortunate as to have landed this mammoth account. My theory is that the folks that made the decision saw what they liked (us) and decided to move forward without the gauntlet of hurdles one usually has to endure when dealing with very large firms. Kudos to them!!

---

7. Clients that allow you to earn their business starting off with trial runs. There are some folks that do it the old fashioned way – they let you earn their business by giving you a chance. This has happened several times in my life and, any and every time it has happened, it has been a good thing for me. I feel that, beyond the various sieves that people put up in carrying out the vetting process, the true test of the pudding truly is in the eating. There truly is no substitute.

   When I start out talking to a client, I tell them that I am interested in getting their business but only a small portion of it. Instead of some revenue producers who aim for a self-confident air such as stating that they wanted "all their business" or "half their business", I tell the client that I just want five to ten percent of their business. That's all. It is realistic because the process of starting out with someone is very tricky. You really don't know what their needs are or their style of doing business. With this initial lack of knowledge working against you, it would be catastrophic to win a very large piece of business and promptly fail in the process due to lack of familiarity and knowledge.

   More potential clients should give the companies that they are interested in an opportunity to work on their business through a sample run. This would give them a true and accurate picture of what the vending partner can really do. This seems rare nowadays in light of what I have seen. Pity.

Clients, especially potential clients, are a tricky business. There are times that you have to listen beyond what is said. The omission of things or things that are left unsaid are sometimes clues as to what the client really is thinking.

Personal Case Citing: What Was Left Unsaid

I was once waiting for a client at his office. The meeting was to be at 2:00 pm but it was already 2:15 pm. I usually give late clients the same rule of thumb that restaurants give late guests of reservations, 15 minutes maximum. Oddly, I waited till 2:35 pm and just as I was about to leave, my potential client, Billy, shows up very apologetic and very flustered.

He apologized profusely and told me he is usually very punctual but things came up and so on. Billy then said, "Well, let's talk about you and your company (the security consultancy) and what can you folks do for me."

Normally I would launch into questions of who they were and what they wanted out of security, etc., but this time I took another tact.

John (J): "I was wondering, why were you late?"

Billy (B): "As I said, I was held up because of some matters that came up. But enough about that, let's talk about you."

(J): "Please, I want to know, why you were late."

(B): "Come on, now I told you what happened. Can we drop it?" Noticeably upset now.

(J): "Sorry, what I meant was what caused you to be late?"

(B): "If you mean what caused me to be late it is because I had 12 regional managers running the global security of my company but a month ago they laid off 4 managers and now I have to work with 8 security chiefs doing the job of 12! That's why I was late!"

(J): "Oh, wow! Okay, now I see."

(B): "John, they won't even let me hire any fulltime replacements because they don't want to have all those long-term costs due to budget cuts."

I sensed an opportunity.

(J): "Did you know that we have an embedded employee program?"

(B): "A what?"

(J): "A program wherein you can have someone work for you but they would be our employee. Hence the term 'embedded employee' program."

Billy seemed interested.

(B): "Tell me more."

Had I not asked a very simple question and persisted, I would never have known about this latest turn of events at Billy's company. Why? Because Billy didn't equate his problem as something that my company could solve. He looked at us as a security consultancy and not as a problem solver of his personnel issues.

There are a myriad of reasons why people make their buying decisions. These are just some of the situations and thinking that goes behind some of them. The key is to perceive where the client is going in your discussions. Is there genuine interest in you or your product/service or are you just another vendor to them? How you answer that question will determine your ultimate success with the potential client.

Chapter 17:
The Real Role of Procurement

This chapter is the shortest one in the book and that is done purposely so. I wanted to highlight the fallacy of the role of sourcing or procurement departments in the process of vendor selection. Procurement is to vendor selection as human resource is to hiring people. I draw that analogy because they both do something that is counter to what you would think they do and that is to pick vendors and/ or hire people. In fact, quite the opposite occurs. People get sifted out by HR departments and companies get eliminated by procurement departments!

If you think that procurement departments are your best friend in getting selected, then think again! They are there to eliminate all but the companies that will fit their narrowly pre-determined templates. So even if you have a whiz bang product or setup or whatever but you don't quite fit the metrics, then guess what? You probably won't make it.

If that seems surprising to you and against the grain of the capitalist foundational thinking, then you may want to examine the basis by which procurement departments operate. The idea of procurement is to standardize what they purchase. Or more specifically, their goal is make their purchases so homogeneous and so predictable that any variant from their templates (even if it is sublime) is suspect as to acceptance. Now, don't misunderstand. I am not saying that, even if a superior product shows up that exceeds the set template for performance or price, then it is automatically rejected. But what I am saying is that the procurement department's job is to look for replication of results not only in one vendor but multiple vendors due to fear of failure and ease of swapping out should one vendor fail.

The other factor that exacerbates the effect that procurement has on the buying process is that they are usually not well informed about what they procure. The operative thinking is that you, as a procurement person, do not need to know the product or service very well; just the process by which to acquire it. The product or industry knowledge can be completed by operational people who are there to fill in any knowledge gaps. In theory this should work; however, I have seen so many RFPs that are structured as explained and have been abominations of mish mash. A case in point was an RFP that asked us (a security consultancy) of what degrees of error (plus or minus) that our unit was prone to fail or be inaccurate. This is laughable because the RFP was floated out to acquire investigative services. Unit? Degree of failure with a plus or minus stated in percentages? Ridiculous! Someone forgot to inject reality into the situation.

Another absurd RFP asked us to quote a rate matrices for protection work in "hot zones" (or very dangerous places in the world due to war or crime). Looking to get the best pricing, this company treated protection work on a "minimal thresholds of safety" basis -- something that we never did or ever will!

Procurement has become a means and an end to itself. In more and more organizations, they wield ever growing power and sway. A lot of times the requesting department or division wants a new product or a new service rendered and they shudder at going through the process of procurement. One time, after our successful bid to gain a global company's worldwide business, the director of the requesting/awarding department took out his pen and was about to sign the contract when he looked up at me and said the following: "John, don't screw up please. I don't want to go through this process again if I don't have to!!" He said it not as a threat but rather as a plaintive request.

Some procurement folks understand their true role and that is as procurer of things. However, when the procurement process goes wildly wrong is when the search for cheapest and the lowest endangers the original mandate to get the best "value".

One such tool of Satan is the reverse auction bid. The summary of this insidious invention is this:

1. Every bidding vendor participates in an anonymous electronic format by keying in their bid for selective services that they are interested in offering to the buying firm.

2. The parties do not know who is competing but they do see the bids of what they are offering to get the business and also that of the other unknown bidders. The "reverse" part is that the bidders are encouraged to offer lower and lower rates with the ultimate intent of being the lowest bidder!

Isn't that fun?! Grown men and women subjecting themselves to this exercise in humiliation and folly! One of my colleagues said that he worked for a nationwide video rental company who put their company uniforms out to bid in this fashion. My colleague noted the glee in which the procurement people were watching the rates tumble. They were "high five-ing" each other with gusto! Why? Were they thinking of all the benefits that would be derived from these savings to the company? No! Apparently there was an incentive program that gave the procurement folks a bigger bonus should the rates fall below certain levels. In other words, these procurement people were incentivized to get the lowest rates possible!

The net effect, after a few months passed, was that the procurement people got hefty bonuses and the winning vendor's uniforms were found to be terribly inferior and had to be replaced with a better made and more reputable firm's uniforms.

Savings? Where were the savings? The value? To whom? You be the judge.

Chapter 18:
The Truth About Contracts

One of the greatest fallacies that exists under the old type of thinking is that contracts are supreme and dictate the tenor and the pace of a relationship between the two contracting parties. Let me say this as plainly as possible: the true binding power of a contract is only as good as the willingness of the vested parties in keeping and honoring the contract. Sure, lawyers and lawsuits are a powerful inducement to follow the letter of the contract, but let's be very honest with ourselves at this juncture. Could a fleet of lawyers make you do anything beyond the "letter of the law"? Can the best written document force two unwilling parties to work amicably together for a very long time? Would you not be able to find a crack in the most "airtight" covenant if you really are searching for one? Lastly, could the best Park Avenue lawyer make you exceed the contract terms to work in the spirit of cooperation and innovation? I think the answers are obvious.

The Contract = Relationship Fallacy

The true core still comes down to an Honorable Relationship -- something that American society seems to have forgotten. Instead, what is sought after and coveted are contracts. Hence the millions upon millions spent on highly paid attorneys and consultants to help craft the "perfect" contract. Don't misunderstand. Contracts are important in that they help to spell out the terms of engagement between two or more parties. The contract document helps to delineate who does what, when, where, and in what manner. However, as a document that binds parties to provide the tasks or services or products, it is only one part of a successful equation. The other and very <u>indispensable</u> part of the equation is a solid and honorable relationship. When the two are present, then you truly have a very strong working model. However, even in the absence of a written contract, business is still conducted all around the world and done so every day with pennies or millions at stake (and it has been done this way for many, many generations.) Done, I might add, without the "suits" to iron out the language of a document. Done without codicils. Done without addendums. Done without anything but the agreement of two or more people. And if anything should go wrong in terms of performance or results, then there are no subsequent lawsuits or arbitration boards. Wow! Where is this near-mythical land of no contracts?

Look about you and you'll see that it is done every day in every country inclusive of the US. This may seem surprising but in actuality why should it be? Did you have the neighborhood boy sign an iron clad contract to have him begin mowing your lawn? Did the boy, in turn, hire a team of legal eagles to make sure that he was not going to be shortchanged should there be a work change order? This may seem amusing, but I hope it is illustrative of the fact that in the prosecution of living, we make many, many contracts and yet none of them are written down. But then you may counter by saying that in business, where there is so much more to lose, the need is there for contracts to spell things out without ambiguity and to anticipate foreseeable contingencies. Of course, I am in complete agreement.

However, I propose that the modern 21st century contracts (and I have been privy to many) have drifted deleteriously from these primary functions in a dramatic way. Let me illustrate. These contracts go much further by:

1. Anticipating any and all contingencies to the benefit of the contract writer or

2. Tipping the advantage to the contract writer (whenever possible) including penalty clauses for the other contract partner

   (The contract writer is usually the more powerful of the two parties, of course.)

Is this a good contract? Is it a "perfect" iron clad contract? If you think so, then I guess you would be on the contract writing side of the table and not the other side. But know that the other side is doing the same as they jockey for superior positioning. This usually ends with some amalgam of the two interests.

But there are problems with this overwhelming dependence on contracts to spell out everything. The first problem is reflected in the old adage "a contract is only as good as the paper it is written on". In other words, the people and organizations (but principally the people) that are behind the agreement are the true determinants of whether the "ironclad" contract is truly one that will be honored in harmony or be contentious throughout the life of the contract. Suspect allegiances based on only mutual "needs" are dubious because, once shifting economic circumstances make these "needs" no longer attractive, how long do you suppose that the "ironclad" nature of the contract will last?

The other problem is this -- will a contract <u>motivate</u> the parties to not only perform to the levels required by the contract but go to the next level of cooperation and collaboration? Doubtful. You can write all the SLAs (service level agreements) and KPIs (key performance indicators) into a contract but UNLESS you have a fundamentally strong and communicative relationship, there is no impetus to unleash true collaboration and innovation. That is the difference between a great working relationship and one that just covers the basics.

All parties involved must realize that the <u>relationship</u> between you and your client is truly the <u>"contract"</u> that binds the two of you. The relationship is what defines the interaction, trust, and credibility of the two parties more than any paper contract could ever do. And that is as it should be. It has been this way from the very beginning of time when people found that working together created a better world for all those concerned than if they only worked by themselves. That was why and how civilizations were built, wasn't it? That is also the reason why we have contracts. To work together toward mutually beneficial goals. This is what makes the process of living more fruitful and more productive.

Yet we have made contracts (which was always meant to be a document of recordation of agreed upon terms) the end all and be all in defining how we are to work together. The contract's place in the business universe has been elevated too high. The contract has taken on a life of its own by replacing relationships in how it defines the interactions of the vested parties. The shame of it is that the contract document is just that - a document. No matter how well written in terms of specificity and detail, it can never cover all contingencies and be as fluid as well-built relationships. Contracts are ill-equipped to foster creativity and innovation. And as such it limits and confines the thinking and actions of the vested parties. That is a very bad thing because it stifles the necessary interplay between the parties that is so essential in coming up with better-than-status-quo results.

Bad, Bad Contract Types and Other Realities

Modern contracts have many flaws and really bizarre outcomes as well. Keep your compass pointed to true north and don't be swept away by what the "masses" may come to believe is the norm. There are some fundamentals that EVERY contract should have. If they aren't there, then run (don't walk) run away! Such as:

1. Stakeholders must have "skin" in the game – something to lose. Listen, does it make any sense that when you sign on the dotted line of a contract, you have effectively hermetically sealed yourself from all harm, liability, or risk? Does that 100% guarantee exist in real life at any juncture in ANYONE'S life? No? Well then why do corporations or attorneys think that they can write away risk just by strong arming someone into signing a piece of paper that shoves all blame and reparations over to the other side? Sure there are folks that have signed (are signing) these types of egregiously one-sided contracts, but how committed are they to these documents if they go bankrupt or do a hit/run type of relationship, casting their fate to the wind hoping upon hope that these punitive clauses will never be activated? That sunny optimism is like living near a toxic waste dump and hoping that you won't be adversely affected by it!

   To be a real working document representing real business relationships, all parties must share some risk. That is a truly sustainable scenario, not the one wherein monolithic companies by sheer size and volume of business bully their "partners" into submission by accepting terms that are intolerable.

   What terms am I referring to? Here are some: unlimited liability, knowing your proprietary secrets, no-knock audits, SLAs that are very punitive, net 120 days, etc.

   Let's review them quickly:

   A. Unlimited Liability – yes, I have truly seen a contract that was written which stated that if ANYTHING went wrong, then we (the selling party) would assume ALL liability and risk without limits! The General Counsel of my security consultancy approached the lead counsel of a potential client (a national telecommunications company) and asked that to be amended to put a cap on the liability (say $10 million). The lead counsel of the potential client said no because this was an acceptable request and other vendors have accepted these terms without pushback. My General Counsel said that no amount of money that we could possibly make would warrant us to take on such are risk as the possible downside would be the end of our company. Furthermore, my GC said, if others signed it then they either didn't understand the real risk behind such a clause, were fools, or were willing to make a fast buck and go bankrupt (eventually) just to win the contract.

B. Knowing your proprietary secrets. There are these copious documents that very large clients have requested seeking to know all of your company's private IT and networking systems. Why? The cover story is so they can be assured that if/when you handle their data, it will NOT be leaked out to the outside world, that you have enough backup systems, encryption, firewalls, etc., to fulfill their requirements. Now, while that may seem like a perfectly "reasonable" request from buyer to seller, the question is begged – what will the requesting company do with the information that they get from their vending partners? What is the level of safety and assurance that the requesting company can offer?

C. No knock audits. The ugly twin sister to the knowledge of your proprietary systems is the "no knock" audits. This is a clause that permits the requesting company to conduct audits on an unannounced basis. This clause empowers them to physically go to database centers or co-location facilities where servers, routers, and networking equipment are stored and to do physical inventorying or testing.

D. Punitive SLA (service level agreements). These are clauses that tie your performance to pre-established standards and levels that, if you fall below them, will have you pay or discount heavily the price you are charging the client. Much like the electronic reverse auction bids, this is a terrible practice that somehow has become accepted by doting (or doltish) companies so eager to sell their souls as to consent to such larceny. The operative thinking is that you (being the seller) would be so eager to do business with the client as to self-flagellate yourself should you lower the standards even if it is just once. Actuarial tables being as cruel as they are, the probability is firmly stacked against such companies that consent to such idiocy.

E. Net 90, 120, 180 days. WOW! This really takes the cake. Not only is a company supposed to render their product/service to the buying company at a thin margin pricing with punishing SLAs and a contract that pushes for unlimited liability should something go awry, BUT now the selling or purveying firm must carry the buyer's purchase by three months or longer. Think about this scenario. If you carried out this practice as a bank that lent out money for homes or cars, then you would not be solvent for very long as your debtors took their sweet time to pay you off. When you finally do get paid, the time value of the money just went into the toilet. Add to that scenario the very possible twist that a complaint or defect may arise that the buying company may raise for non or partial payment.

2. Contract stakeholders must back each other up. Every business minute of every business day, foolish companies sign on the dotted line knowing full well that they or the other vested party may not or will not live up to the spirit or the letter of the contract. This level of disingenuousness is further proof that the business world is truly spinning off its rocker! How can anyone go into a contract with the idea that it will not be honored? Doesn't that defeat the purpose of the contract concept? If that is the case, then all the lawsuits in the world would not compel either party to comply. This is breaking faith in the worst way and that is to know with aforethought that you will never be able to live up to what you said you would in writing. If you think that this doesn't happen every day across the business world, then think again.

3. A contract in other countries is seen as the starting point. This point is something that most Western (i.e., US companies) don't quite get. In countries around the world, whether they be in Europe, South America,

South Asia, Middle East, or Asia, the contract signing is just the beginning of the business negotiations (inclusive of pricing) and not the finalization of them. This is something that I stumbled over a few times in my early work in international waters. I was raised in US society and was taught that the signing of the contract was the culmination of negotiations and talks and evidenced the cessation of these activities. Now it was time to carry out the contract! Or so I thought. But now, looking back at the various nasty surprises that came from doing work in Asia, I found out that the contract signing didn't end the dealings involved between two companies but, rather on the contrary, it signaled the intent of these entities to move forward with more seriousness in working out the pricing, terms, and conditions of the inked document.

The concept is akin to the process of negotiating or haggling over purchasing items overseas. In the US, when going to the supermarket, it never even crosses the mind of the buyers to haggle with the supermarket owner or manager over the cost of the T-bone steak that is proffered for sale. This would be met with strange looks and possible calls for their security staff to escort you out.

Americans aren't used to this type of arrangement and generally don't like to haggle for things. Consequently most Americans are not good at negotiations as a result of this cultural distaste for the activity. It is a blind spot that needs to be corrected because that is not how the rest of the world operates.

In almost every culture outside of US or Canada, the market conduct doesn't loathe negotiating even after contract signing. The purchase of food, clothing, cars, or anything is subject to this haggling. It is a type of sport much like fencing with its thrusts and parries. Don't misunderstand. A lot of US firms and business people are catching on and even getting very good at it; however, they are still a small minority compared to the vast number of entities and people that do not know about this sobering fact of doing business outside of North America.

The three previous examples were cautionary in nature but the following example is actually opportunistic in nature.

4. People hate the contract process – use that to your advantage. No one that I have ever met, done business with, and carried long term business relationships have ever said the following:

"Gee I love doing contracts. They are so exhilarating and fun! I wish I could do them all day long!"

All of the people that I faced off with on opposite sides of the bargaining table told me (after the contract was signed) that they hated this part of their business activities and that they sincerely hoped that I would live up to their expectations because they really did not want to go through this process again if they could avoid it!

The arduous nature of the work behind contracts has been cited as being a major factor in making sure that everyone involved is miserable (even procurement people)! Once again, why? Because contracts in the modern world (especially in the US) are so painfully crafted to create a painful scenario for all signatories other than the contract writing company, of course. This simply is ridiculous.

Sub Section: RELATIONSHIP

Now that your knowledge of yourself and your client is clearer and you possess a better understanding of the real life use value scenarios, the next step is to work on relationships. Armed with knowledge of self/client and use value, you are able to undertake relationships at a much deeper and more actionable level.

Essentially, beyond what has already been written in previous pages, there remain two elements to relationships. Both involve interactivity between you and the client and in both cases you must be the initiator.

Chapter 19:
Following a Series of Permissions

The ability to build a strong business relationship isn't all about "chemistry" or "filling needs", though they do play big roles. It is about the correct way of approaching a new client. This chapter highlights how to go from "out to in" in a way that allows the client to pull you through their maze-like world that may be fraught with potential land mines.

It is important to know that advancement with a client is achieved through a series of permissions. Acknowledging and using the series of permissions is a very important step towards developing a long-lasting and profitable relationship. Moving from introductory permissions to intermediate permissions, and finally to the mature permission stage, you will find that moving along this continuum will deepen your relationship and build trust more effectively.

Much like when you are getting to know someone, would you ever (unless you were socially inept beyond all belief) say things like the following after having known them for one hour?:

"I was told by my friend Jim that you really are very kind and loving. Would you consider having a baby with me?"

"Hey I know I just met you but could I borrow $5,000?"

I don't think so. But rather the relationship, whether platonic or not, begins in what I call ever tightening concentric circles. You start out at fairly neutral ground and move ever so slightly and gently through a slalom course of questions, answers and observational opinion making (on both sides). Based on the replies and the "chemistry" that may come of all this, you and the other person may start to realize whether there is interest on both sides to meet again and deepen the relationship.

It is foolish to think that you can "hotwire" the relationships quickly so as to cut to the core and get intimate in knowledge, physicality, or anything else. No, there are no shortcuts in this process. Consider this: would you want someone you just met to be as brazen as the aforementioned two examples? Probably not, I would wager. A relationship, shallow or deep, is built on a series of permissions. That is to say, a series of permissions from both sides to progress further. This is a fundamental building block of relationships.

There is nothing more excruciating or amusing (depending on your bent) to listen to a person being shot down by someone else because he/she was too presumptive in their approach as to the level of engagement that other person was willing to share/go.

Personal Case Citing: Eavesdropping at a Tony Restaurant

I was having cocktails with my wife one evening at a very posh restaurant and bar in Toronto. We were having a real fun evening when, unbeknownst to me at the time, a couple sat down behind me. I would never have taken notice of them beyond a glimpse if it weren't for the fact that their conversation became, well, sort of distractive.

I tuned in to hear a conversation that went like this:

Man: "I am so glad we finally got together! It's great to see you finally in the flesh as it were. I thought about what you looked like over the many times that you and I conversed via the Internet."

Woman (slightly flustered but feeling complimented): "Oh, gee, thanks! I appreciate that. You look great yourself."

Man: "Yeah, I mean it's like I've known you for a long time especially as of late when you were talking about all the stuff you've gone through lately."

Woman: "Yeah, it's kinda creepy how much we know about each other, especially considering the fact that we have never met!"

They both laugh at this juncture.

Man: "I gotta be straight with you on this. I really, really dig you. I think you are very kind and warm and loving and I am just bowled over by you."

Woman:" Th-th-thank you."

Man:" I really want to take this relationship to a whole other level."

Woman: "What do you mean by that?"

Man: "Well, I think it would be cool if we could maybe be physical if everything works out well for tonight and beyond."

Woman: "Oh, um, I don't know. It's kinda rushing things a bit, don't you think?"

Man: "Now, listen, in this world there's way too many things happening that get in the way between a man and a woman and I think that that's stupid. I mean, we both really like each other so I figure, why not?"

Woman: "Well, I appreciate what you are saying but I am still kind of seeing Brian as I told you."

Man: "Oh, him. Yeah I know but come on! How long are you going to keep the light on for him when you've said countless times how much he's hurt you and how you want to start afresh?!"

Woman: "I know but..."

Man: "Listen, he's simply no good for you. He's demonstrated that fact over and over again, hasn't he?"

Woman: "Yes, but after all, I've known him for many years and it's easier said than done..."

At about this time, my wife had noticed that I was not paying attention to what she was saying (not a good thing overall) but when I had indicated this incredible discussion going on behind me, she and I both (shamelessly) tuned into it further. As a consequence, I missed a few exchanges but when I listened again, this is what I heard:

Man: "I don't know why you are still going out with that loser. I mean it's not like you're ever going to be married to him."

Woman (very tense and upset): "Th-th-that's not for YOU to say!"

Man: "Well (pause) I just think it is ridiculous! I've got a lot to give. And I've gone out with A LOT OF WOMEN and they loved it. I've gone out with some of the most beautiful women in the world. Did I tell you of this one Italian model who was runner up at the World Beauty Pageant......?

Without recounting the whole horrid chain of events that came from this terrible tactical change in approach, needless to say, the man and the woman parted company relatively quickly with a very tense and awkward goodbye.

I give this citing because it was almost laughable in the way the man handled the situation; laughable only if it was not so painful to listen to and the empathy we both felt for the woman as he trampled over her feelings in his clod-like presumption of the level that they were both at. He was dead wrong obviously but we can learn from this scenario in our business dealings.

Business relationships could be just as awkward and painful as what I just related to you. A very real error that a lot of so-called salespersons make in their approach to client is their assessment of where the client is at versus what they really are.

In order to avoid this happening to you in the business world, it is best to develop the relationship with a potential client from day ONE. One very powerful way is to do the necessary homework on the client and his/her company prior to the meeting. Get a baseline for the relationship by doing some research on them and their structure, mission, and overall corporate culture. This can be done very quickly in the age of the Internet. However, don't assume, as the man in the citing, that you know the company or the individual from what you got over the Internet. This is, after all, the "official" position of the company and not what it may truly be in real life.

The next phase is done at the initial point of contact – the first meeting. Be a gentleperson, ask neutral safe questions such as size of company, main product lines, etc., when meeting for the first time. True, you may already know some of the answers, but be receptive to aspects you didn't know from looking at their website. When making any major statements about that company, if you feel compelled to do so to prove that you know who they are, ask them if what you said is true or still true.

Another way to look at the situation is to study the shark and its approach. (Please suspend the negative connotation of sharks.) Seldom does a shark (even if it is three times your size) attack you straight on without warning. The shark is a primitive eating machine but it is very sophisticated in its instinctual methodology of attack. The shark does elliptical circles around its victim. It starts from a point far away and it tightens the circles as it gathers data. Data? Yes, it is finding out more about you. It will brush against you a few times to see what you are like. Furry? Scaly? Tough skinned? Spines or stingers?

The shark's skin has millions of neural receptors picking up these signals and determining very quickly if you are a prey that might strike back and hurt it in the process of it trying to eat you! Once the shark has determined, to a certain level of satisfaction, that it will not be harmed by trying to devour you, it will come in with mouth open and eyes rolled back.

But you are not a shark and your aim is not to devour or even hurt the target (person) but rather your aim is to know more so that you can get to deeper layers of knowledge and familiarity/comfort that you are establishing with the potential client.

This is not a Machiavellian exercise wherein you will be using this information to harm/hurt the person but, on the contrary, it is done so that you will, through a series of questions/answers, comments, opinions and observations get to know if the person is receptive to allow you to get more information from them about themselves and their organization.

Another less menacing illustration would be a person entering a maze through doors that are opened by the potential client if he/she shows that they have their client's interest at heart. The salesperson is allowed to go from the outer maze into the inner sanctum through progressively more and more sensitive doorways.

But unlike the insensitive man in the previous citing, you don't barrel in with your pre-conceived notions or agenda. You gently but firmly move forward seeking tacit or overt permissions of the potential client to move forward. Each phase becomes progressively more intimate but it is solely dependent on the potential client ALLOWING you to come in further.

In all my years of selling, this process does not happen in one session or quickly. It happens with time but, dependent on approach and receptivity of the client, the process happens very smoothly and well if great respect is shown and acknowledgement that these mile markers of intimacy are not taken lightly by you.

There is an unwritten rule that 80% of sales are either consummated or fail by the fourth physical meeting. To move progressively closer to acceptance by the potential client, you must move along the "Permission Spectrum". Here's what it means:

> Stage One – Yes, I will listen. The client is willing to listen to you and hear your points and your approach, all the while determining if it is good for them to allow you to continue.

> Stage Two – Yes, I will share. The client is willing to tell you information about themselves, their organization or their needs/challenges. This step is crucial. It is pivotal in terms of getting the client to open up with crucial information so that you can proceed further.

> Stage Three – Yes, I will agree. The client allows you to move forward to discuss, carryout or go to the next level of engagement.

Key things to remember as you engage with the client:

- Ask questions and map out what their world is like. Pretend that you are a blindfolded and you are feeling out the interior of a room. With all the furniture, pictures, and objects in the room, you need a guide who will help you to "figure out" the layout of the room.

- Pick and choose areas of exploration based on feedback given by the client. There are some areas that you may want to explore based on your needs or speculation; however, if the Client Champion does not want to go there, then respect their decision. Broach the topic only when you think the Client Champion will not have "a problem" with your question.

- When engaging the Client Champion in areas of interest, ask who else is vested and might be interested in this type of work. It will help to know who else within the organization may also be interested to take on a project similar to the one you are working on with the Client Champion or who else you need to get "buy in" from in order to move forward.

- Present ideas or thoughts for the client to consider. Ping them to establish if there is interest in moving forward or if there are other things abrew that they have not yet revealed.

In summary, the ability to move closer and closer with a client comes from judicious and appropriate overtures and information sharing. Anything else would be ill timed and premature which usually spells disaster as far as being shut down or deemed impudent. The road back to grace, if one is offered after such a debacle, is a long, hard one.

Chapter 20:
What Makes a Brand?

Creation of a personal brand is key critical to any business relationship; not your product or your service or your company's brand. Your brand. You. Simple as that. But why you? Why not sell the company or the product/service? Because people don't buy from machines and they don't buy from companies; they buy from people. People buy from people. Especially if it is a big transaction worth a lot of money and if it has tremendous upsides and downsides. They buy from YOU!

Branding yourself, that is, making yourself into a distinct and highly desirable purveyor of good things and good service, is really where most of us aspire to be. The trick is to be able to attain that coveted status with a loyal group of high paying clients. Want to learn? Let's go to it...

First, there's some definitional work we have to do such as what makes a "brand"?

A brand, in my estimation, is an entity or mark that has something that no other "peer" type entity in the market has - **customer loyalty that is not impeded by price. That is to say, customers are willing to pay a price higher than for similar products in the marketplace.** It is a very hard to achieve this goal but I have done it and so have others. So can you if you haven't already done so.

Second, what are the characteristics of a successfully branded product? Successful brands all share the basic commonalities:

1. Consistently exceptional quality. Brands don't become brands by being middle grade and they certainly don't become brands by being inconsistent. In a way, the latter is worse than the former because a middle grade brands can also flourish (e.g., Denny's). Not to single out or diminish Denny's, but no one goes to a Denny's for haute cuisine. They go to Denny's because the "Moons over My Hammy" in Augusta, Maine are the same shape, texture, smell, color, consistency and ultimately taste, as the ones that are served in Shreveport, Louisiana. Consistency is key.

2. Not too broad a scope of products/services, but a well-developed and created product family. Brands have iconic products or services that no one can do quite as well. That is what helps to establish a brand over others. Consider the Swiss Army knife which is a unique invention but one that also has had many imitators throughout its storied history. The Victronix brand is unique in that, while it makes variations of the Swiss Army knife with certain attributes, the product's functionality, color scheme and look are very, very distinctive.

3. Brands need to keep their product line fairly tight and not diversify too broadly. Mercedes Benz in late 1990s to mid-2000s was highly criticized by customers and professional automobile writers for creating too many models. With the "S", "C", "D", "E" classes, they had many sub category vehicles with a wide range of pricing from very expensive to moderate to fairly affordable car pricing spectrums. It could be argued that Mercedes Benz had gone a little too far in the "being everything to everyone" mentality. The idea of brands is that it is "not everything to everyone".

4. Has a distinctive style, look, or delivery. This is part of the mystique of a famous brand. The way it looks separate it from the rest of the pack. In design, structure, or delivery, the look of the product is what they have capitalized and promoted. Here are some famous examples:

    Tiffany's - little pale blue box that has the recipient's heart skip a beat upon viewing

    Burberry – toffee colored plaid pattern recreated in a thousand permutations!

    Absolut Vodka – distinctive bottle shape (supposedly an old Swedish medicine bottle)

    Ferrari – flowing and curved lines – like a curvaceous belladonna with over-the-top dramatic colors

    Tumi – the notched zipper handles and clean and industrial lines of their cases – connotes all business

    Coca Cola – one of the ultimate iconic shapes – the bottle shape that can only be Coca Cola

These firms take pride in their ability to conjure feelings and emotions of trust, satisfaction and even snobbery because they have carefully crafted these feelings in the public mind/heart by years of products offered, advertisement and customer experiences that reinforce these emotions.

4. Appeals to a higher-end market (not looking at price but emphasis on something else) – aiming for elite decision makers. All the sales, marketing, design, and delivery of these products and services are all aimed at higher ground. Not happy with the mid-tier or lower markets, these brands strive to be the best in their categories. There is always this mantra of:

    Age or Experience – from 1820 (or whatever date the firm started), they have toiled to bring the best to you because they've perfected the process throughout the decades

    Perfection – by painstaking manufacturing process, experience or hard-to-find materials, the brand is able to bring the best quality to you with an unstinting eye for quality

    Rare – hard to find and even harder to attain. If you want this product or service, then you better be able to pay for it and be patient in acquiring it!

    Fashionable – an emblem of being hip and cool and at the forefront of being sleek and highly coveted

    Appeal to Elitism – this is not for everyone. It never was meant to be. If you don't have a level of discernment due to knowing the level of quality, engineering, or difficult, deliberate processes that it took to create this product, then you obviously don't deserve this product

    Worthy – not only is the product worth acquiring, but you must be worthy of owning it!

A lot of snobbery and elitism isn't it? However, it truly works!! This type of thinking capitalizes on the human need to stand out. The need to be different makes people do things in extreme just to show the world their uniqueness. Consider the bizarre conundrums of: 1980's pony tailed mid aged white business men, 2000's obsession with tattoos especially with young and mid aged women with a design or comment above their buttocks ("tramp stamps"), and the equally obnoxious pierced body parts of the 2000's. All these symbols of individualism seem comical especially in light of the wholesale adoption by masses of people. After a while, it can be asked that if everyone has these symbols of their uniqueness then how unique are they really? Nonetheless we all strive to be "different" and "unique" and if a group of product can help in being a differentiator then people will embrace them!

5. Tells a cogent and compelling story about your product. Sometimes products or services have allegorical tales surrounding what makes them so unique to begin with. Hospitals and clinics are advertising very heart-wrenching yet touching stories of how patients come in (at a point of death) and because of their expertise, they are given a new lease on life.

    Mercedes Benz and Land Rover tell stories through advertisements and word-of-mouth of their legendary resilience and stamina. In their advertisements and their sales language, there is a constant drum beat of strength and dependability. Volvo touts its safety features and even goes so far, in one TV advertisement, as to talk of Volvo co-founder's wife's influence on him as he was designing and building the cars (apparently she was in the medical profession and cared greatly abut health and safety).

6. Presents a strong message that is told consistently. Notice the advertisement of companies such as Accenture, Microsoft, and SAP in the airports of the world. These firms know that a lot of people frequenting airports are business travelers and, while the travelers may not think of these companies' products when they see the ads, the advertisers also know that the consistent subliminal "white noise" of their ads tends to create a familiarity. By sheer repetition of the message to the mass of folks moving through, the advertisers hope to create a sense of knowing and comfort in the target audience. If you doubt that this is a conscious plan, then look into the cost of running just <u>one advertising campaign in one airport for one year</u>!

7. Creates an industry buzz. Long before social networking and the heavily touted benefits of that phenomenon, the master brands of the world knew how to tap and use the landscape of opinion makers. The brands capitalize on people that other people look to guide them to what is "cool", "fashionable" or "attractive".

Whether by endorsements from movie actors, athletes, or famous celebrities, these brands know how to influence or co-opt the masses by pivotal people's views. Or they use pivotal events such as:

   a. Equality movements (Virginia Slim's "You've come a long way baby" cigarette campaigns aimed at the feminist movement of the 70s or NAACPs long running "A mind is a terrible thing to waste" campaign)

   b. America's space program was mentioned in the old Tang ads because that's what the astronauts drank

8. Provides an opportunity to test the quality of the product and learn more. High value brands want you to see what they are all about and to pull you into their world. They want you to "buy" into the image and mystique of who they are and what they make.

There have been thousands of advertising copy pages written extolling the virtues of what a company's products can do or how it is made or what it is made of or how others simply adore the product! The underlying premise is that the more you read and understand the product's superiority, the more you will accept the proposition of paying more (and sometimes much, much more) for the product than its industry peers.

So all these commonalities tend to be found in the high value brands and their attempts at distancing themselves from the pack. If you accept this as true, then the natural question to arise is why is all this effort expended to create this distinction? What are the benefits of such a strategy?

The benefits of branding are very palpable and powerful. The brands that have established dominance in their respective fields enjoy these wonderful results:

More profitability. The markups of clothing lines with a coveted fashion label are astronomical! Think about it. Most of the clothing is made in developing world markets and sold to developed markets - think of the pricing differential between COGS (cost of goods sold) versus the retail prices in tony stores such as Neiman Marcus, Bergdorf Goodman, Saks Fifth Avenue, etc. The markups are HUGE!!!

Greater longevity. Brands live a very long life maintained by the old guard buying them who, in turn, indoctrinate their young ones to the joys of the product. Patek Philippe advertisements trade off of the father/son legacy. Also, consider such storied old brands as Abercrombie & Fitch that has literally re-invented itself from a stodgy-your-grandfather's store to an over-the-top hip, loud blaring music retailer with half naked men/boys plastered on their walls as you enter their stores. Quite a departure but the actions of the savvy business managers of A&F have saved and revived an old brand to pre-eminence! Brands have the ability to instill great loyalty, and that is why they may last for hundreds of years. They keep consistency while they iterate with the times. Think of old brands such as: Procter & Gamble, Coca Cola, Gillette, Chevron, etc.

Heightened attention from the market. Major brands also attract attention from media and markets worldwide. The activities of Apple, Facebook, Google are very closely watched not only because of their economic impact but also because they tend to be trend setters in how they do business, forge into new areas, and innovate to create new products and services. The markets in any period of time and any area always look for bold leaders to create products or markets that never existed. That is why leading brands hold a fascination that follower types can never really capture. It's easy to copy but it is hard to blaze trails because the chance for failure is always imminent and high!

Increased growth in margins and market share. These are the key drivers in any business but especially with very high marquee brands. The ability to command higher margins in the face of the constant, almost overwhelming drumbeat demands of clients/customers to lower rates, is what makes these well branded companies such incredible anomalies. They tend to fly against the fate of mere mortal brands with lesser market powers. Why? Because the perception, real or otherwise, is able to pull the clients in regardless of what conditions that the markets are gyrating to.

How can the aforementioned characteristics be used by you to create your own brand? This is a very valid question considering you don't have the luxury of generations of clients following you and a gargantuan advertising budget. However, you can leverage what these firms do in your own approach to clients.

Chapter 21:
Creating Your Own Personal Brand

Branding can be done very effectively by knowing the approach you will use with what you have. You must critique realistically your company, its capabilities, yourself and your capabilities. You cannot try to be something you are not, so don't even try. The emphasis is on creating a branding vehicle where the client "gets it" about you and your company.

There are things you have to put into conscious motion, and it starts with an assessment of what you want your clients to know you for. Here are some initial things you can do to establish your "brand".

1. Pare down offerings to true core competencies. Sometimes you don't have this choice but you know that there are certain things your firm does well and certain things that is simply not its strong suit. This can be easily gauged by talking to the Client Champions who will tell you whether you are on the right track or not.

2. Offer the best product/service within that niche of core competency offerings. Don't feel compelled to offer everything that your firm has to give. If you have a killer application, then see how it would work beyond the normal applications and industries. Is there anything that you can foresee (or are guided by) that may be a very important iteration of your company's core competency product or service? Innovate with the client to create new offerings or new usages of old offerings. It is not hard. Really. Think it through with the client as to what are other areas where your company's product or service may have other serviceable attributes for them.

3. Aim high and court aggressively, but not obnoxiously. The key is to shoot high once you do the preliminary homework on the client (see Chapter 11: Homework) and leverage relationships to get into the inner circle of the targeted client (see Chapter 12: Leveraging the Power of Multiples and Chapter 14: Developing the Client Champion). By leapfrogging past the competition, you will be able to get to the inner circle of the decision makers fairly quickly.

4. Create your own style, look, method, and way. There is a line, hard to draw for some, but nonetheless a line that is distinctively you or what you project but does not go into areas of unprofessionalism. I have seen it in many different forms. Some mentioned are:

- Starbucks card sent to break the ice or make people feel good

- Personalized after-visit cards that thank the client for their time and consideration

- Working on committees of associations and contributing to the overall effort

- Organizing events to showcase or spotlight an industry's interest or concern which the company is highlighting

- Newsletters that may be distributed (though this is very difficult to do on a long-term basis due to its need for consistency)

People tend to think that branding is an expensive proposition; however, it really is not. It requires thought as to what image or approach you want to create. Then move forward with the concept. It may not be "perfect" if it is your first foray into branding, but you should try it to see where it will lead you.

6. Create the image and reality of complete coverage. Something very vital to every client relationship is the idea that you are their advocate, that you care beyond any of the competition or even their internal personnel about the client's welfare. This is something that doesn't happen overnight; however, there are things that can be done to cement this type of advocacy imaging. And it is real, not just an image. Here are some ways. I call them the five "I's":

Instruct the client – Tell them who you are and what you do, as well as what you want to achieve with them. Lay your purpose, products, and goals out in layers – be the consigliore to the client in "Godfather" terms. Too many times, vendors want to hide what they really want, which is downright foolish. Why not make it clear to the client that you want their business and that you will work hard to get it? It is not naïve. What is naïve is to pussyfoot around about your intentions.

Insulate the client – Give them no cause to leave or look elsewhere. Concentrate on taking laborious tasks or functions away from them, helping them to concentrate on their core competencies. The more you can make the client's life easier, the more they will draw upon you to help them. I've seen this happen time and time again.

Psychologists call this "referent power" in that the client refers to you for all matters related to your field. In my world, the most cherished words from a client are "I don't know if you can do this but..." or "I was thinking about something and would like to pass it by you..."

It is all based on making the client come back to you again and again and draw from your company's products or your work/expertise.

Inoculate the client – Admit to your weaknesses, but also correct those weaknesses quickly and effectively with a network of people who will be able to cover the needs you aren't able to meet. Talk about strengths/ weaknesses of the competition and honestly assess your standing in relation to them. Be careful not to overemphasize these points.

No one is invincible and there are times when you will fail; however, recover as quickly and as honestly as you can. (See upcoming section called "Flawless Execution".)

Involve the client – Work with clients on projects that will involve you both in solving problems and creating new answers. Involving the client allows you to learn the internal architecture of the client's world. Get in the trenches and do the "hard work" with and for the client. There is nothing like working on a project with and for a client that will help to bond the relationship between a client and his/her vending partner by stress testing it and seeing where the strengths and vulnerabilities may lie for the client and his organization.

Knowing the internal workings beyond the various facades that you or the client may put forth is something that you should pursue.

Innovate with the client – Present new and different applications of your product, drawing inspiration from clients, competition, press, and your own experience. Propel new ideas and create favorable circumstances or catalytic events to encourage forward movement. How? One way is to ask the client if there are problems that continually plague their company, issues that may not be "burning" but are nonetheless the perpetual "pebble in their shoe". Or present various scenarios that you have worked on with other clients and what resulted from them.

Another approach is to address the bigger issues of the client's world, not just what is immediately at hand. Sometimes the client is so wrapped up in their world that they don't see the things that cause problems on a macro level. Your insight may lead to new projects or reference power

---

Case Citing – Wine and Water

The wine industry is another indicator of the power of branding. There are so many wines out in the market, from so many countries, from so many years that is truly overwhelming in terms of volume. And yet, only select brands can command the premium prices.

Lastly bottled water would have been a laughingstock of a concept if it weren't for the phenomenal revenue it generates! What started out as a cottage industry has exploded to phenomenal volumes and revenues! An estimate by the Beverage Marketing Corporation shows US bottled water for 2011 as: 9.1 billion gallons and approximately $11 billion. [20]

Remember the forces at work in Chapter 2: The New Strong Forces in the Business World? Well, they are making you and your company a commodity and not a brand. How can you reverse this trend? The effect should be to tailor an image that is very difficult to tarnish or diminish. The Honorable Relationship consists of:

A. Superior Knowledge of client and environment

Your knowledge of the client and your ability to address their concerns/ initiatives/problems establishes your "brand" with the client. Mapping out the client better than the competition, or even more than the client will consciously allow, creates uniqueness. Knowledge not only of the obvious or expected, but also of the client's nuances, will give you and your company a competitive edge. Sometimes it's not a matter of intimate knowledge but just knowing the context that the client is working in.

Personal Case Citing: Knowing Where the Client Lives

My company was competing to get the business of a very large French energy company that wanted to have its employees and partners vetted for criminality, credit checks, and anything derogatory as part of its initiative to bring more of their in-house operations under compliance.

We were one of three firms that were auditioning for the business. The selection committee consisted of three Americans and three French compliance managers of the client. The meeting was held in the US east coast so the three French employees flew in for the meeting. This is the same meeting that I attended that I asked the French contingency if they worked in the "Black Rock" located in La Defense portion of Paris which really helped to break the ice.

After a short presentation by the French contingency as to whom they were and what they were looking for, it was our turn to do our presentation. My sales director did a great job presenting the facts of what we could do for them as we went through the PowerPoint presentation. I sensed as I was watching the group that we were doing a nice workmanlike job but we weren't burning up their world. I felt that we needed to do something to get their attention!

At the end of the formal presentation I got up and made my summation statement. I said:

"Thank you for giving us time so that we can get to know you better. I know that there are two other firms that you will be looking at to judge whether they are worthy, same as what you are doing with us right now.

I realize that this is a form of a beauty pageant (to which they smiled and chuckled) and that we are all putting our best face forward to impress you. However, when you sit down and consider which vending partner to go with, I would like you to consider the following about my company:

You cannot outgrow us – we are at all the major markets

We are experienced – we've been doing this type of work for 150 years!

But the most important thing that I would like you to remember more than anything else is…"

And that is when my voice trailed off for a second and I saw the selection panel leaning forward.

"Ready?" I teased them. Some of them smiled.

"You will never see your name in the headlines because you hired us. We are very careful."

It was then that I saw a few of them scribble furiously in their notes I deduced that their main emphasis was to stay out of the news and that was what was driving their whole initiative in checking on the backgrounds of employees and partners.

We won the bid.

B. Anticipatory service

This type of service is so uncanny that the client can't experience the level of service coverage from anyone else because it is just that good.

Examples from my personal experience are Singapore Airlines with their superlative friendly service coverage and Hampton Inn with their little touches (such as a workstation caddy for the bed!)

What is it that makes these firms so good at what they do? I think it is the fact that these firms look at their product and industry from the vantage point of their customers. What is it that the customer wants? And how can they be satisfied without the purveyor going broke?

I find that when I give service to the client that exceeds their expectations, it is usually when I help them navigate through their own world. How does that work? Here are some examples:

Ease the sourcing or requisitioning process for your clients by making your response easy to read or helping to craft the RFP

Offer compliance assistance to help them get through industry regulatory requirements

Provide enhanced communication for the client in the form of reports or dashboards

Link or streamline services to multiple parties within the client's organization

Offer services that come from very specific and internally driven specifications – tailored offerings

Service that anticipates what the client wants and not off-the-shelf in format will differentiate you from the rest of the pack like nothing I know. It is what helps to build trust and create loyalty.

Personal Case Citing: When Love Made the Sale

There was another bid tender that I was a party to but I was not as actively involved as other projects. My task was to open up the presentation and give closing remarks. I really didn't know what my role was because another department of our company had done all the work. And it was a lot of work - about five inches of RFP response!

This bid tender was different because our company was the incumbent. In the session planning meetings, I saw the level of dedication and planning that went into the presentation. So much so that it made me realize that there was a lot at stake here. The client was a very large NGO (non-governmental organization) which had a worldwide span and was very demanding in their requests for real time information.

This department was given a mandate from our president that they must not lose this very valuable account. I was told to help with the presentation and work some "magic" to retain the client.

The day of the presentation came and we were in front of a five-person selection committee. I began by introducing the team and their roles in the presentation. The team members took it from there and did their part in presenting what they had done and what they would do in the future.

As I studied the faces of the five-member selection committee, I tried to figure out the approach. It was kind of too late because we were already well into the presentation; however, I thought that I had a good angle.

When the last team member finished speaking, I got up to do some closing remarks. I started out by thanking the selection committee for listening to the very detailed presentation with earnestness. I pointed out the fact that I was personally impressed by the volume of work and attention to detail that was invested into this RFP response. Then the following ensued:

"You know, folks, it is a double edged sword to be the incumbent in an RFP situation! Unlike the competitors (who have no track record with you), we are faced with the daunting task of keeping your interest with us in spite of the fact that the new guys probably will have promised the moon to you. You have seen us fail and make mistakes. You have seen our warts and blemishes; in short, you have seen us without our makeup whereas the competition is fresh, new and full of promise!

"Therefore it is very easy to fall into the line of thinking that new is better simply by virtue of the fact that they are sexy and new. However let me remind you that through all this data, statistics, facts and figures, there is one thing you should keep in mind as the main differentiator between THEM and US! Do you know what it is? (Pause) L-O-V-E" (I purposely stretched out the pronunciation of the word.) I got really quizzical looks from the panel!

"Yes, ladies and gentlemen. We are saying we love you." (I got some chortles and embarrassed smiles from the panel and my team for that.)

"Why else would we devote so much time, energy, and effort if it wasn't love? Why would we work on initiatives so quickly and respond so speedily if it wasn't for love? Why would Samantha (my company's team member) take calls from Cara (NGO member) as late as 8 or 9 pm if it wasn't love?" (Now the smiles have vanished and very contemplative looks flashed onto the faces of the selection panel.)

"In summary folks, please consider wisely your choice of who will be the next vending partner for your organization. The pull of the sexy and new is irresistible but temper that with the dedication, competence, and love of your original partners. Thank you."

We won the bid. I am not attributing the win to what I said, but I can't help but think that it helped to re-focus the thoughts of the NGO selection panel on what was important (flashy consultese wonk-speak or people who would walk through fire for them).

C. "Flawless" Execution

In this world of overblown hyperbole and the myth that a lot of companies try to sell you regarding their flawlessness or their state of perfection, one can easily be drawn into thinking that the best companies never really make mistakes. Or at least the kind that most mere "mortal" companies make. This is as far from the truth as East is from West.

Every company, and I mean every company, has issues and problems that they would rather not have to admit to or deal with. However, it is in the dealing with these problems that separates the truly great from the want-to-be-great. The aforementioned statement is not an excuse to constantly make mistakes or to do poorly with the aim of eventually doing well. No, on the contrary. It is an acknowledgement that even the best organizations on the planet are subject to factors that are either beyond their control or are within their control but still not able to overcome them. What these exceptional people and companies do in the midst of situations that go wrong or horribly wrong is what makes the difference between a fair weather relationship and a relationship of solidarity able to withstand the punishments of time, tide and circumstances between them and their customers.

Case Citing – The Lexus Recall Story

This case has been cited by others before but it bears repeating to underscore the idea of "flawless execution".

When Toyota Motors began its Lexus line in the late 1980's, the operative thinking was excellence. Excellence in engineering, excellence in design and excellence in execution. And as the world and American press kept on drumming that message into the minds of the American public and the American car makers, a growing resentment began to percolate in the American car companies of the seeming infallibility of the Japanese (especially Toyota).

So it was a great schadenfruede moment when the Lexus line had to recall some of its initial cars due to wiring and brake light issues. It could have been an HUGE black eye event because of all the hype that surrounded the Japanese TQMS (Total Quality Management System) and its highly vaunted perfectionism. However, the Lexus folks, knowing that a lot of the world was watching as to how it would react, did the right thing. They didn't point fingers or try to explain away things. Lexus had the recall and they did it with aplomb. Servicing of the recalled cars was done with such speed, ease and professionalism that the affected Lexus owners were even more impressed and sang the praises of Lexus even more so had the event not occurred![21]

The concept of flawless or perfect execution is just that - "a concept". You can Six Sigma and TQMS (Total Quality Management System) a plant, process or company to death but the hard reality is that there will be fall down because we are flawed creatures that live in a flawed world. The other ugly reality is that these fall down events and how you react to them determines the relationship more than any contract. If you project the idea that you or your company have all the bases covered all the time, then you are only tempting fate as the probability game will be against you. Sooner or later, you and your company will foul up and make a mistake (maybe even a big one).

As part of the five "I's" that were delineated earlier in this chapter, I put it to you that you must not create a false sense of invincibility but rather to "Inoculate" your clients of your humanity and the possible fallibility of your organization. Obviously, one must not over-emphasize this point too much so as to be your own worst critic in shining a spotlight on an Achilles heel that needn't be emphasized; however, a healthy dose of realism as to what you are able (or not able) to do is good.

So let's say you drive into work on a sunny day and you are feeling very wonderful about your place in the world. You go to your desk and find that your voicemail box is full. As you listen to the voicemails, you have the sinking feeling that your earlier state of euphoria was misplaced. Something really bad has happened during the night and to top it all off, your Blackberry or iPhone was out of commission so you were not able to address the issues on a real-time basis.

Your co-workers are screaming at you for resolution even though you don't have the full picture of what happened overnight. Did I tell you that this debacle happened to your best and largest client? Now, what do you do?

My suggestions, having encountered enough of these situations to fill two large volumes of an encyclopedia of gaffes, are as follows:

1. Find out (as reasonably accurate as you can) what happened

2. Find out who was affected and to what varying degrees of damage or loss

3. Find out possible fixes. Preferably two or three really plausible and realistic solutions

4. Talk to the Client Champion regarding the problem and the possible fixes

5. Talk to the client decision makers using information and guidance that was given by the Client Champion

Let's examine the progression of thought and action in the aforementioned sequence. There usually is one of two gut-punch reactions when something bad happens. One is to hide or blame something or someone and the other is to immediately fess up to the problem. While the first is more natural (even though more craven), the second one is not necessarily the best initial step. You see, apologies are alright but solutions are better. Your approach with the client needs to be contrite but informative and problem solving as much as you can possibly be.

While apologies tend to salve initial anger, if you do not have real solutions, then the client will wonder if you really know what you are doing and/or if you really have the situation under control.

Once you have a pretty good assessment of what happened and who/what it impacted, the next step is to formulate fixes that will cauterize the wound. Whatever you come up with should be technically and physically feasible or else it will come off as grasping at straws in terms of fixing the problem.

The next step is crucial – present the problem and the fixes to your internal Client Champion to see if it passes "muster". This is important because sometimes, due to your lack of knowledge of the client, you may proffer ideas that, while totally realistic in its approach and feasibility, may in fact be completely at odds with what the client is willing to permit. This is predicated on the thought that you have the time to do so but usually you do not have that luxury.

After consulting with the Client Champion and weeding out the fixes that won't work, it is time to call the person who is answerable to the screw up in the client organization. Paint the picture with details that will give him/her a realistic picture without giving overly flowery detail. How do you make that differentiation? Judge it by what you would absolutely need to know about a situation which would accurately portray what happened. Then apologize. This is very important because the natural reaction to such bad news is anger, frustration and/or disappointment.

Then proffer the shortened list of possible fixes that were vetted by you and the Client Champion with your recommendation of the "best" possible fix based on feasibility, cost, time, etc. Then shut up.

Listen and take notes with special emphasis on where your client decision maker is focusing on in terms of their perception of the problem and their opinion of the fixes offered. If they ask questions, answer quickly and fully. Based on their feedback, acknowledge it and give approximate feedback on answer or solution of the problem. If it is a complex issue, give possible phase 1 and phase 2 handling of the problem.

The key to all this is speed and confidence but with a measured dose of humility, so resist (at all cost) defensiveness. Now, if the client doesn't let go of the problem and keeps coming back to underscore your failure, you may need to have a level set that all organizations make mistakes but that yours is doing its level best to fix it. Recriminations are not going to solve the issue at hand. Look him straight in the eye and DO NOT BACK DOWN while staying professional and polite.

Personal Case Citing: When Love Keeps the Sale

When I was working for the telecommunications giant in their voice and data division for business clients, I was very fortunate to have met a fellow who was the IT/communications director of a fast growing software company. His name is Lyle and he had an acerbic sense of humor borne from many years of working in a high pressure environment. Yet, through all that cynicism, he is deep down inside a truly nice guy.

I was working on switching him and his company from one voice/data carrier to my company's system. He was receptive and, after a few tweaks, we moved forward to signing a contract. I double checked with our provisioning and delivery department technicians that the more than generous two weeks that Lyle allowed was more than enough time for them to do the cutover from the other company's system to ours. When I delivered the new contract for Lyle and gave him the assurances I got, he took out the pen and was just about to sign it when he looked up at me. Lyle said with a half-smile but with all seriousness the following "John, I trust you, that is why I am doing this. Don't f**k me!" I was taken aback by that statement but I acknowledged that this would not happen.

During the two weeks of provisioning, I checked many times with the technicians to see if we were on track for cutover on a particular Sunday night at 8:00 pm which was the slowest time for Lyle's company's network usage.

Sunday came and Sunday night at 8:00 pm came. I was waiting and had my phone on. 8:05 pm – nothing. 8:11 pm – nothing. Then suddenly I received a call at 8:12 pm with a very anxious Lyle calling to tell me that the old carrier's system was cut but ours had not come up on the grid yet – his network was dead. He said "John, don't f**k me" in reminding me.

I quickly hung up and called the lead technician and tried to find out what was going on. Beyond all the technical gobbledygook, what I got was that they ran into some physical limitation issues because the plans that they had for the system didn't match the physical configurations that they encountered when they tried to do the hard cutover. I was stunned. I asked them, "What do you mean 'the physical configurations that you encountered'? Didn't you look at the physical grid and equipment during the two weeks you had?"

"No, we were working off the plans..."

"WHAT!!!?? You mean to tell me that you never really looked at the physical guts of the company's system and only worked off of drawings????"

"Y-y-yes but I..."

I didn't let him finish. I swore and tore into him. As unprofessional as that was, I really didn't care because a major betrayal of trust was revealed in our provisioning department.

"When can this be done?"

"10:00 pm tonight – about 2 hours from now" was the answer.

"You sure?" I asked.

"Absolutely."

I called back a very angry and concerned Lyle with the newest deadline and while he wasn't happy about the situation but it was still Sunday night.

I waited until 10:00 pm. Then at 10:05 pm, I got a call from a furious Lyle saying "John, you are killing me. You are literally killing my career in this company. Are you happy? I won't have a job because of you and your company!!!"

He wasn't kidding. Lyle's reputation in the company was going to suffer greatly if it wasn't going to be fixed.

I called back to the lead technician and was told the mind blowing time of 7:00 am on Monday morning (a work day!). My jaw dropped! I really didn't want to tell Lyle but had to. He was almost sobbing.

It is at this time, I would like to tell you that everything went well and that the system came up at 7:00 am or at least near it before anyone came to the office. I can't because it didn't. I had a terrible night of poor sleep and knew that Lyle probably regretted the day that he met me, much less gone with me and my company.

I called the technician and said in as controlled of a voice as I could muster the following "Listen, you've been giving me deadlines and not meeting them. All the while the customer hates us and thinks that our word is crap! I need you to really, really tell me the truth when this system is going to come up!"

"11:00 am" is what I heard and my heart sank.

"Will you do it by then, truly?"

"Yes I absolutely promise" the technician was choking up because he was feeling the stress of disappointment and frustration.

"Okay."

I took a deep breath and picked up the phone to call Lyle with this latest and hopefully last update.

John (J): "Lyle, I am so sorry and I know you have heard it all in the last twelve hours but I gotta ask you something."

Lyle (L): "What what what!" (He was perturbed beyond belief)

(J): "I need to ask you a question. And the question is this – do you love me?"

(L): "What???"

(J): "Do you love me?"

(L): "Is this some kind of messed up joke? What do you mean: 'Do I love you?'"

(J): "Yes, do you? Because the answer I have to give to you is based on your answer."

(L): "I don't know what you mean by all this..."

(J): "Do YOU love me as a human or a person or know that I have tried to do well for you but that I have failed? Please indulge me and say whether you love me or not."

(L) (very tired): "Okay, I love you, okay?"

(J): "Thank you. I love you, too. And people who love each other don't purposely try to hurt the other person, do they? Please know that I have done and will continue to do my best to make you believe, trust and love me. The new time is 11:00 am and I promise you this. I will fall on the sword for your boss and your bosses' boss when the system is up and we will eat the first month's billing."

At 10:50 am Monday morning, the system came up and I got a phone call from Lyle ecstatic.

(J): "Hello?"

(L): "I love you! The system is UP! I love you, man!" (His voice was cracking from over-tiredness.)

(J): "I love you too, Lyle! I know you've been through a lot with me but know that I am always in your corner and will always be there. And if I screw up, then I will fix it!"

(L): I know that now! I know that, man!"

Even though that experience was as painful as being dragged by wild horses through a field of broken glass, it did make our relationship very, very strong! After that, the account calls (physical and telephonic) were all very convivial and pleasant. When I left for the US east coast looking for a new career, it was Lyle that I asked for a reference and he gladly provided it!

You see, at the end of the day, it's about whether you give a damn about your client and if you are willing (failure upon failure, trials and travail aside) to work HARD to make them well and whole again -- if you are going to work for them and be their friend and advocate. If you are, then you will gain a friendship and a bond that will be extremely difficult to break. But if all hell breaks loose and you go into panic or (worse yet) blame mode, then you have done something that will destroy any chance of recovery.

The irony of these very troubling and always–to-be-avoided scenarios is that, if you recover well enough, they actually can act to elevate your status and your standing with your client. Whether in the form of war stories or what-not-to-do allegories, your client may chide you for the screw up but ultimately they will respect and work with you as never before.

Sub Section: EXPLORATION

Chapter 22:
Leadership Vortex

WOW! We covered a lot of ground thus far. We've transitioned from Knowledge to Understanding Use Value to Relationship and now we are moving to the summit of business relationships – the acts of Exploration.

In Exploration, the main ingredients are that of working collaboratively to solve problems or promulgate initiatives that the client seeks to address but cannot or will not do without a trusting relationship with a true partner. I know that "partner" is such an overused and maligned word, much like "solutions" or "synergy" or "empowerment". However, if you really have gone through the stages of Knowledge, Understanding Use Value, and Relationship, you will truly be at the sweet spot of a business relationship (and consequently a fun spot to be in) called Exploration.

There are two main areas that must be considered in order to truly plumb the Exploration Phase. One is the Leadership Vortex and the other is the Stewardship Compact. Let's work on the first one right now.

Much like a relay racing team, the development of the Leadership Vortex between you and the client is one of running the race faster and better coordinated than previously thought imaginable on an individual basis. The operative premise is that two very well-seasoned and trusting teammates will be better suited to solve problems and hurdle obstacles than one lone performer.

It starts with how to initiate a Vortex and the client's role in the Vortex and the ultimate outcome of this very different way of client partnering and collaboration.

Utilizing the Leadership Vortex

Now that you have worked hard with the client to get to this point, most people would just simply be satisfied and just dwell in the Relationship Phase. I guess that's okay if you want to just stay at a certain level and go no further (in relationship and revenue). But I think that you are looking to create a very strong competitive advantage that will be very difficult to knock down by the voracious competition or the gyrations of wild markets!

You see, only staying at the Relationship Phase, while not necessarily hard, is really limiting. And if something stagnates, then the law of atrophy kicks into gear so that it becomes increasingly hard to keep the status quo of relationship and revenue because you are constantly being challenged by internal and external forces to prove each other's worth. These forces will ask "What have you done for me lately". This is not a tenable situation in the long term.

The Leadership Vortex is increasing performance between you and your clients (and even internal constituents!) by a dynamic that evolves from working collaboratively with the client to not only address issues currently at hand, but also work together toward future projects.

Why do I call it a Leadership VORTEX? Because, like a vortex in space or earth, it has a characteristic of pulling things into it and as you get closer to the center, the objects move and spin faster, faster than it would by itself.

So what are characteristics of the Leadership Vortex? There are three cardinal components:

1. **Baton Passing of Leadership Role.** This is achieved by constantly alternating the leadership roles that you and the client will play for each other. Much like runners in a relay race, the baton of leadership is constantly passed back and forth between you and the client to urge on the efforts for improvement.

    Note: This is a complex relationship component because it requires coordination between the client telling you what they want and your solution as a response to their request. However, clients alternate between wanting to tell you how things are to be done and wanting to be led by you (because of their lack of expertise or vision of outcome).

2. **Working on a Big, Ugly Current Project or a Huge Future Project.** This is key in that if there were no wheel to grind the axe onto (so to speak), the axe never gets sharpened. The baton passing of leadership needs to

work on a mission or project that supersedes the present and move into space that has not ever been tread upon (or at least not successfully). The partnership needs a crucible by which something new can come out of the intense heat and effort expended to create a new product, system or entity. To work and solve a big project to the satisfaction of some of your best clients is a HUGE competitive advantage!

3. **Fresh Flow of Ideas.** If your relationship with the client is a body, then this would be the blood that delivers the oxygen to the cells! Drawing from only your industry as a source of new or fresh ideas is poor in terms of the vast wide world in which the free flow of ideas is constantly refining and hybridizing new thoughts, approaches and paradigms. Ideas can come from you, the client or anyone of the camps on either side of the fence. It can come from outside world via media, consultants, universities, ground swell movements. Creating intercompany task forces or projects is a surefire way to create challenging new ideas or answers to previously "unsolvable" problems.

How can you start this Leadership Vortex? To begin with, you must initiate it and in order to do so, you must be able to have double vision – the ability to see two views. You need to wear two lenses in order to enact this phase – one that is your viewpoint and the other is that of the client's viewpoint.

Let's begin with a healthy assessment as to whether you are truly at this stage of Exploration. The question is not of longevity or how much revenue you have gotten from the proposed targets for your next phase of work. While they may be good indicators of possible Exploration candidates, these are not the benchmarks you should use. Rather, you should see whether or not you are at the right levels based on these criteria:

- Good flow of information and a level of comfort between you and client to exchange ideas

- You have worked on small, medium and large projects with this client in the past and if so, were they successful?

- The client fundamentally trusts you and your company to the degree that he/she is willing to work on new or sensitive projects

If, in your assessment, you think that you are "there" with the client, then move forward. If in doubt, ask him/her – no problem with that at all.

So let's say you are there. Now what? The three aspects of Leadership Vortex are covered next -

Your Participation, Client's Participation, and Use of the Leadership Vortex.

Your Participation In the Leadership Vortex

It is essential to offer leadership early on in this phase of the rollout of the Leadership Vortex. It is incumbent on you to "paint the picture" of what you would like to do with the client based on discussions of the past and from anything that comes from dialoguing with the client. At this phase, there is no "selling" involved. It is merely to query the client as to what are some medium- or long-term goals that he/she would like to achieve.

1. Offer ideas and innovations to the client. Projects usually come as a result of one of two things:

    a. A problem or dissatisfaction with current conditions which necessitates a need to change the process or system so as to effectuate a better model of doing things or accomplishing core functions of the client's company

    b. An emerging market, product or need that the client company needs in order to lead or maintain the lead that the client would like to have

NOTE: Even if these are initially shot down, they may lead to other projects and ideas. Sharing them early will help to bookmark this interest so that, when needs or circumstances change, the client may be able to revisit the issue with you.

"Ping" the client about different areas of application, or people that your product/ service would be of further value. Identify new uses within the client's world and who might benefit from these new applications. The idea of re-purposing comes into play. Keep in mind that products and services must iterate either in form/

function or application. If the client can utilize your product/service to do their work better, or if they can use it in heretofore untried ways, then these ideas should be on the table.

Example:

Remember in the examples given in Chapter 2 of the basket-making company (you) and the client? What if you had talked to a client that sells their products using baskets (of which you are a steady supplier) and you wanted to talk about how you can do new products? Here's how it might begin. Let's say the client has always wanted to break into selling more of their products to new types of customers in other markets. Their current presentation utilizes a straw-based basket format (which you currently provide); however, the line is getting stale and so are the revenues from it.

Perhaps a format to increase share with new markets might go this way – how about presenting a packaging that sells in regions based on regional differences (whether it be in color, construction, or format)? Could the usage of red baskets in China or Chinese-based markets be of value? Yes. Why? Because the Chinese culture utilizes red as a basic color scheme throughout its culture. It is a color of cheerfulness, cultural identity, and comfort, as opposed to white, which is usually a color of death (as black is in Western cultures).

Or maybe the materials used are no longer straw or wicker but perhaps synthetic or recyclable materials which may conform to concerns of "green" thinking. Thinking in terms of materials sustainability may be attractive to the sought-after customers of the client.

Or maybe shape and usage of the baskets could be altered so they can be used for other purposes beyond just a conveyance of the client's products. Think Coca Cola's iconic bottle look and shape or Absolut Vodka's distinctive bottle design. Could the basket shape, construction and color/texture be used to promote the brand image of the client's products? Sure it could.

2. Communicate your intentions clearly to the client. Work with the client to clearly define what you are trying to achieve. Using the example given, have the client understand that you "get it" based on the history and discussions that you have had with them. You understand their

thinking and what they are trying to accomplish in breaking into new markets and finding innovative ways to get their products to stand out, in not only form but also function, that your ideas will help to bolster the image and revenue of the client. This can be done in a myriad of ways:

A. Lead by example (what you can do) – give conceptual drawings and approaches. Do mockups of some proposed ideas of the various types of baskets that might be offered. Give them examples of what your company has done for others in their similar situation.

B. Lead by faith (in your vision) – give a clear, unambiguous message to the client that you and your company have been very vested in the client's best interest historically but that you want to take that relationship to many levels higher by being of greater value in terms of offering more innovation, creativity, enhanced performance for their product line. Nothing is more consoling and confidence-building to a client than when his vending partner is thinking of new ways to be of greater service to them.

C. Lead by co-opting talent (Power of Multiples) from your company or even that of outside consultants who can add to the idea generation phase by their unique skills/backgrounds/experience/education. The formation of an intercompany project team (the client's people and your people) can be a great starting point – explanation later.

D. Define what it is that you are seeking from them. In one word – participation! Are they willing to invest time and personnel toward this effort? If they are, then great – half the battle is won. If they are not, then find out why. There may be many factors: no budget, no time, no political will, etc. The worst of the list of reasons is "lack of political will". The budget and time issues are usually smokescreens or a lack of vision to see that a lot of things really don't have to cost a lot or take a lot time/resources. If they work under the idea that beginning a discussion is the first step and see where it leads, then that is enough! If they aren't even willing to talk , then forget it for now. Ping them later. Or never.

3.   Seek their guidance to achieve your goals. What are they telling you? Even in their objections and limitations, you can learn a lot of the roadblocks that may be encountered. Remember, you are not smarter than the folks you work with; they are privy to a lot more information and political gamesmanship inherent in their company than you will ever care to want to know! However, the perspectives that you bring from working with similar clients allow a visibility to the client's situation that transcends its company's limitations or even its industry. Your basket company expertise in various industries and companies allows you a visibility to possibilities that the individual client companies may not be able to see simply because your activities cross many lines (industries, world markets, vertical markets, etc.).

Listen and weigh the client's advice carefully because they may be telling you things you may need to know about a project. If they are pulling their hair out and have gone through many iterations of the solution (with other vendors), then there are two distinct possibilities. One is that they cannot see past the problems internally and don't get "it". The other is that the other vendors have not understood the complexity or political/structural roadblocks that need to be navigated. Hence the stalemate. Notice I did not say anything about the IT, technical or physical aspects. Those usually are the least of the issues preventing solving a problem. Sometimes problems are insoluble because of the nature of the organization and its people politics that, more than anything, blocks problems from being solved. Why? Maybe the solutions involve a large amount of changes – changes that might affect personnel, head count, reporting structures. There may be multiple parties racing for the solution within the same company and, in the process, each team may downplay or even try to sabotage the other team's efforts. Whatever the client is telling you (or not telling you if you sense this) may be very important signals that you don't want to miss in the mad dash for answers to "solve" the problem.

4.   Propose alternate routes if met with negative responses or offer ideas and innovations to the client that you have done for others. There are always roadblocks on any project. It is the successful company and

individual that can hurdle them by equal parts ingenuity and persuasive skills. What do I mean by this? Consider this. Ingenuity may come from thinking of the problem beyond the actual physical or financial limitations – it may involve company culture and thinking. If this seems to be the issue, then you must consider how to highlight that these changes (if adopted) will affect the outcome of the company in a very positive way, even though it may change certain departments, divisions or business units. If the dollars and cents of it doesn't register into the client company's psyche, then perhaps an examination of whether the key decision-making players are receptive to this type of change is necessary. If they might be receptive, then what might their drivers be (remember the iceberg illustration of the various uses in Chapter 8 that the buyers are trying to achieve such as political, financial, strategic, or operational). It may seem manipulative and it is; however, it is for the ultimate good, is it not?

5.   Invite the client to think of new or different applications for your product/ service. What does this mean? In the context of what your product/ service has to offer to the client, what are areas and functionalities that your company can offer which will enhance the client's world? Examine the needs that the client has. Are there areas in which your company's products can be extended or stretched or innovated to fill needs heretofore unmet?

Personal Case Citing: A New Practice is Born

In working on reviving one of my company's flagging divisions in Asia, I was struck by the fact that the Asia division was clearly out of touch with the changing nature of the Asian economy (especially that of China). The people, thinking and market approach was still working under a model that worked in 1995, but certainly not in 2012. The business that we had done so well in was anti-counterfeit work and we had worked it very well; however, in the recent decade plus, the mark had moved and we weren't aware of it. As a result, I took on a campaign to dive deep into the market and what the companies that were our current and potential clients were trying to tell us.

The results were quite eye opening. The anti-counterfeiting work that my company was so famous for was still valid but it iterated to a much higher complexity and need as the counterfeiters were becoming much more sophisticated with multiple country operations and becoming a lot smarter in hiding their operations. Not only was this a factor, but also the bad guys weren't just satisfied in imitating or copying the originals (our client's intellectual property); they now were aiming at theft of secrets to their benefit. Stealing formulas, algorithms, strategic plans, customer and channel partner databases, etc. was the new order of the day. This was the backdrop by which the clients were confronted on a daily basis. The bad news was that we didn't understand this. The good news was that neither did our competition (at least that is what my understanding was).

This was an opportunity of immense proportions if we were smart in seizing that opportunity. So, we have embarked on the efforts of not only bringing our practice up to standards 15 years ahead (that is to say, present day) but also to take it to the next level for the market. What we needed was a multi-disciplined practice called Trade Secret Protection which was a combination of many types of disciplines converging on a company's tradecraft protection.

The early results is a great amount of interest in what we are proposing, and we are currently working with clients to flesh out what that type of protection would mean and entail. This is not easy as each company has its own particular needs and limitations. However, the interest is heartening for us to push forward.

Client Participation in the Leadership Vortex

This part of the Leadership Vortex is very important and very difficult unless you divorce yourself of product or company (your company) thinking. This is the part where you must consider the client's world and perceptions. All the relationship building up to now has been a dress rehearsal for this part of the work.

This part is also counter-intuitive as you must relinquish part of the "go get 'em" attitude that has made you so successful thus far. It is the part of the relay race in which you must give your client the baton of leadership to guide you and your company to the next stage of development.

It starts by allowing the client to guide you where he or she wants to go. **That begins simply with a very heartfelt and deep conversation of not only the physical or logistical ramifications of the project or problem, but (rather) also**

the attitudes, aspirations and outcomes that the client sincerely wants to achieve and how it is to be achieved.

Note: Your goals must not diverge from what the client wants to any great degree. A large divergence will create problems. In the event of a significant difference in objectives, the partnership should be responsibly re-assessed.

This does not mean that whatever the client wants is best. Then you are nothing but a yes-man or toady. No, what it means is that you listen and take copious notes not only of the physical or financial constraints but also of their emotional struggle and even angst that they have. To truly empathize with their situation is key. Remember – this is not just a normal project. It is something that the client dearly wants to achieve and do. It could be the culmination of years of frustration and disappointment that they want to address once and for all. It could be something that could make or break the individual's career involved. If this seems melodramatic and farfetched, believe me I have seen this several times in my career.

Empathy is important but collaboration toward the answers is even better. Steps in the process (in no particular order) are:

1. Acknowledge and utilize the client's strengths and abilities. Chart or map, if it makes it easier, what the client company can or cannot do with the client's help. Is the client currently able to overcome the problem with the resources at hand? Are there enough funds, time, political will (backing) and resolve to pursue the problem to its final and successful conclusion? What are the obstacles (internally and externally) that prevent the ultimate goal from being achieved? Are these obstacles able to be overcome? If not, then what needs to happen in order for this to occur? These are very, very hard questions to ask and they may involve very difficult answers. But asking them and getting truthful responses are critical to go forward on projects of this type of importance.

2. Dig for the client's deeper motivations, which involves discovering what the client is actually saying. Are they doing this just as a half-hearted attempt with little real hope of acceptance or belief that this project

has any real chance of succeeding? If that is the case, then politely but firmly indicate that this is your perception. If they deny such a defeatist attitude, then challenge them to clarify so that you do get an "accurate picture" of what they want to achieve.

Personal Case Citing: When We Won but Lost at the Same Time

Early in my career in consultancy, I lead an effort to winning a very large RFP from a client company that is a huge chemical multi-national firm. We worked very hard in proposing to them the solution for their worldwide counterfeiting problem. It took many departments of my company from around the world to come together literally and figuratively to come up with three iterations of a constantly moving set of requirements and decision makers. We finally were awarded the worldwide solution from the functional heads of the chemical giant! I was, to say the least, very elated.

We started on the first aspect in South America and attacked it with a vengeance. Our efforts were rewarded with great results in our first piece of interdiction which netted counterfeit goods in the kilotons! The client seemed very pleased with the results. Or so we thought. However, as we were preparing for Stage 2 of the enforcement program, we received an odd request. The chemical giant client asked us to propose what we were doing for them to a consortium of chemical giants (an association of sorts). Ever obliging, we proposed as we were requested. However, as I feared, the results received a very mixed response. The multi-headed consortium started to nitpick and go off in different directions, which made me wonder why we were going through this exercise when we had conclusive proof that it worked with the first great results! After a very candid discussion with my Client Champion, I found out that the chemical giant did not want to fund this program by itself. It wanted others to pay for the bill in an industry-wide effort. Well, it devolved and became another form of secondary RFP request for the industry giants. We worked hard to prove the point to the association but it was shelved as the efforts were being diluted by competing companies' competing agendas and egos.

The result was that there was no Phase 2. It stopped cold in its tracks due to this new and unexpected twist. Nothing was heard of this program for years.

3. Analyze decisions and discussions in the wider context of your client's company vision for the future. Sometimes the client can only see through

the lens that they have – the lens of the company's policy, procedures and mindset. There are a myriad of competing and non-cooperative initiatives in every entity so this is no surprise; however, the question is - are they able to see past their parochialisms and move forward to areas that might change how they think, operate and view themselves? If not, then this might be a huge stumbling block in solving issues that might change the client's paradigms. Not all problems can be solved unless there is a fundamental will to solve these problems in spite of the company's point of view, not because of it.

Are they hostile to new ideas and approaches? Ambivalent? Friendly? Impotent? These are all considerations that can determine your ability to move forward.

Preamble to the Leadership Vortex

In the context of what we covered as to your viewpoints and those of your client, and assuming that the field is ready to be tilled, the next step is to move forward with the Leadership Vortex.

I have joked around that some of my best deals were written on the back of cocktail napkins but, whereas it invariably elicits a laugh, it is, nonetheless, true! Not to say that I spend a lot of time drinking while working or with clients but some of the best noodling through times with clients has been to suspend disbelief and budget constraints. There have been times when your client is saddled with so much detritus of their company's limitations and policy that they are not able to get beyond them. However, get beyond them you must!

The vision may start out with a nagging unfulfilled need. A need to, once and for all, solve a problem or make something better than currently available. It has come from the simplest conversations and sometimes in the most subtle of ways such as a sigh or a comment on the hopelessness of a situation. It takes a special person to pick up on these nuances and touches. It is so easy to gloss over and push your agenda or even the agenda of the immediate need or projects of the client.

This is where the relationship that has been fostered (or being fostered) is so crucial. The "if only we had..." or the "can you do this....?" type of comments get me to tingle mode instantly. Remember the barrier to entry (for your competition) is very slight if all you are doing is being better than what the competition is also good at. However, it is a completely different story when you are offering something that no one has either contemplated or has put into place. This rarified atmosphere puts you on the map in so many ways but it is not without risks and downsides. Keep in mind that most of the Leadership Vortex premise is predicated on things that have yet to be seen or even conceived of but nonetheless need to be pursued!

Any time you experiment, you open up an avenue for failure. There are two scenarios which warrant taking such a risk. One scenario is the nothing-to-lose status that you might be in. When you have little or none of a client's business, but have a pretty good relationship with the client decision makers (and there is no foreseeable prospect of that pitiful situation changing due to the strength of the competition), you may definitely consider proposing a daring project based on what the client has mentioned. At the minimum, if you fail, then you have not lost any market share or revenue because there was none to begin with.

The other scenario is that you have a very strong relationship that enables you to talk candidly about issues with your client and explore the soft underbelly of their company.

Chapter 23:
The Leadership Vortex Diagnostic

So the question remains – Now what? Okay, let's see how to approach a client using the Leadership Vortex. There is a series of questions and promptings that need to be answered to see if you have something to work on in terms of the Solving the Ugly, Big Problem or the Next Huge Project.

Question 1: What outcome have you each envisioned?

If you were to take on this project (as a client and as a vending partner), what would be the ultimate result? How would this project make the client's life easier and in what ways would it make it easier? These are very good opening questions to ask because it usually gets the Client Champion to think of utopia and all the good things that may come of such a state. Clients usually get very animated or excited in answering because they probably have invested a lot of time on how their world would be so much better "if only" really became a reality.

Example:

Client says, "I think if we get this done, we would have products go to market in half the time."

OR

"I think if this happened, we would really penetrate the upstream market of this division's sector."

Question 2: What is the scope of your vision?

That is to say, what is the preliminary estimation of the height, depth, and breadth of such a project? This is sometimes the hardest for clients who have been beaten down by "no's" internally so much that they can't conceive of where to begin. That is natural. However, it is your duty to get them to think "blue sky" (no limits) and consider, if they were to undertake this project, what would it look like and how big would it be?

Assure them that this is not a vain and fruitless endeavor because sometimes, in thinking it through with someone from the outside (such as yourself), the "impossible" becomes more "probable". At this stage there should be no talk of what you and/or your company can do. Nor should there be any jumping to "solutions" or methodologies. You are simply gaining information (which should be written down meticulously) as to what the client is thinking regarding the size and scope of such a project.

Example:

Client says, "This would involve the whole Asia Pacific Division's IT department... maybe the whole global IT infrastructure."

OR

"This would involve the overhauling of the whole process by which we do business in this market."

Question 3: Who or what would need to be involved to make this contemplated project successful?

This is an honest assessment that the client <u>must</u> give you to have this project get off the ground, even if some of the people or resources may seem absurdly against or not available at this time. Remember, this is just professional "noodling". Then, very naturally, the client needs to tell you in percentage terms as to who may go along with this.

Example:

Client says, "I need to have Mason, the VP of Procurement, buy off on this and he is probably 60% for such a thing. Then we would need to have Jenkins in the business unit X to say yes to it (he may be 30% for it) and then, if we got past these two, we would need to have the Executive Committee approve it which is comprised of:

President Stimson - don't know if he would back it up – no clue or a "wild card"

Executive Vice President Marquette – she would be a strong advocate – 90 or 100% for it

Chief Operating Officer Smith – she would approve if we could show profit in year 2."

Question 4: Is there political will (inside and outside) to get these projects accomplished?

This is tough. It's the hardest question to ask and have answered, even if everyone was being 100% truthful, because it involves the human heart and the vagaries of business politics and circumstances. I have asked this question many times and have gotten many types of responses from "no way" to "difficult but maybe attainable". In any of the cases, dig deeper to find out why it is "no way" or whatever the response would be. Even if the Client Champion thinks there is political will, then ask why he/she thinks that. The questions to ask usually revolve around:

Budget/Timeline – what is the spend and how would it impact the company? But if you were not to do this, then what is the cost of delay or non-movement? How long will it take to do this project?

Politics – if there is factionalism (and there always is), what are some hurdles and what are the ways to overcome them such as co-opting agendas into this project.

Complexity – the sheer daunting nature of such a project may scare off anyone, but at the heart of it is the next hurdle (see below).

FEAR – the biggest of obstacles there is in terms of getting things approved. Sometimes even the best answers are met with "no" simply because of fear of failure. The question to ask then is "Is the pain of the problem enough to force a solution?" An example is a person with a long neglected cavity in a tooth but doesn't go to the dentist due to fear of pain. I have a friend who does not go to the dentist at all. He has not had a dental checkup and cleaning in DECADES! This is not because of budget or lack of resources. He is simply afraid. However, when he had a tooth cavity (go figure!) that he was ignoring due to fear, which became worse and worse causing excruciating pain, he finally went to the dentist to remedy the situation and eliminate the pain. "NO" is the easiest answer to give, even when there is a lot of pain. However, if there is enough pain, then things will get done. Whether what gets done is a patch/fix, haphazard solution which addresses symptoms and not the disease, or whether the answer is a hard one.

NOTE: Notice I didn't mention the logistics or technical aspects of the project? These are seldom the main blockers.

Question 5: Who is capable of accomplishing the project and its components?

If you get past the other questions, then this tends to be an easier question to answer. Who or what groups would be involved to tackle the issues?

Example:

Client says – "This will take a dream team of:

Jenkins from IT

Derby and Manheim from Logistics

Serrano from Operations along with her deputy, DiDonato

Terrell from Human Resources"

Question 6: What pre-work needs to be done in order for this to take place?

Every company or entity has a protocol and a way of doing things. What are some of the things that need to be done in order for the project to take place?

Example:

Client say,- "We need to put together a proposal that can cover the needs of the project and be vetted by the Operations Committee. If they don't kill it and give us their honest opinion on what needs to be done, then we may have a chance."

NOTE: offer to help in "pitching" this concept to that Operations Committee. As so often is the case, people within a company (even if they are right and are fully qualified) don't have as much credibility as a professional outside of the company. Paraphrasing the Bible – a prophet is not honored in his own land.

NOTE: Designate what pre-work or projects have to be accomplished in order to achieve the ultimate goal(s) and set a timeline and the personnel that need to be involved in order for this pre-work to be done.

Question 7: What process will be followed to accomplish, monitor, and evaluate the progress of each project?

Here again, the client's input is invaluable as to how to navigate past the obstacles and bumps-in-the-road that you will encounter. Every entity has its way of doing things in its prosecution of matters. Learn them. Know what to do and what NOT to do from the Client Champion.

Example:

Client says, "We will need to do this in phases. Documentation of what we are spending in the first three months is critical as my company is very nervous about projects that run amok. We'll be tracking every week by the Logistics department whose head is Thurman."

Question 8: How will your company define success? How will your company define failure?

This seems a little silly to ask, but it is crucial. How does the client's company define these two extremes? Sometimes you can do everything right and still not be "successful".

Example:

Client says, "We define success as having less than two customer complaints in a business week."

OR

"We define failure as not being able to solve the 60-day delay in provisioning of Division X. 45 days is mediocre. 30 days or less would be good. 15 days and we all get raises!"

Please note that the sequence of these questions is not accidental. They are asked in this progression because they take the client through the paces. Why do you want to do this? Besides getting a good idea of what needs to happen for success to take place, it is also a great diagnostic as to the feasibility of such a project in their minds (and yours) before undertaking the task. Paraphrasing the Bible: count the costs.

After this exercise, you and the client can determine whether it has a real chance.

The Practical Leadership Vortex

If you've cleared these hurdles, the next step is to put into practice the Leadership Vortex by clearly delineating the things that needs to be done. Relax. The hard work has already been done if you have gone through the preliminary discussions and The Leadership Vortex Diagnostic. This part is essentially committing to writing the guidelines that you and the client will be operating under.

The process begins this way:

1. State the goals and objectives of this project with specific timelines and budget level thresholds.

2. Map out your participation levels, and assign what you and the client are each going to do. Evaluate the anticipated interplay between different

parties involved in different projects. Basically, you are creating the tasks and roster of folks in both organizations that will be following up on these ideas.

It is critical that both you and your Client Champion be on the forefront of leading this joint effort from the beginning so as to make sure that the mission and goals are met and not sidetracked. It is also important that there are project managers who will keep the projects' teams on point and moving in the right direction(s).

3. State in writing what you and your team are responsible for, and what the client and his/her team are responsible for. This is crucial because, if you don't have this done in advance, it becomes a "he said, she said" exercise when you come to a problem that requires reference back to what was originally agreed upon.

4. Clearly delineate areas of leadership, strength, competency, and natural interest. Be very honest about your respective capabilities. This may be difficult, but honesty is important for both you and the client. Who does what best? It usually is the case (not always) that you bring new skills and fresh perspective to the project (or else why would they go external for help?).

5. How will the end goal of the project stay in focus throughout? How will you and your client stay focused to a successful conclusion?!!

Personal Case Citing: By Land or by Sea

Back in Chapter 10: World Domination Program, I had recounted the Personal Case Citing: Befriending the "Enemy", which talked about my efforts to co-opt a difficult operations manager of the logistics company I worked for. What I hadn't told you was what led to my initiating such a situation.

You see, I had just started out as an account executive for this container ship/logistics company and had done very well on the Pacific side. My office was in Seattle. But what was missing was the highly coveted European Eastbound trade which tended to be very profitable due the fact that the transatlantic trade didn't just ship wastepaper, forest products, and scrap metal (base freight) like the transpacific trade was famous for. I wanted to break into a very big account in the Redmond, Washington area famous for their man-lift equipment. It was a very large shipper of this expensive equipment and my company had zero share.

I approached the operational logistics head of the client, Adam, and asked what we could do to leapfrog past the competition. He stated that he wanted to find a way to move his equipment (in specialized 45' containers) from West Coast to East Coast by rail, and then take them to Europe from there. He wanted to rail them out to the East Coast because the transit time for the shipments leaving Seattle port and going through the Panama Canal was very slow and really causing problems in terms of customer turn time. Adam also wanted to create a competitive advantage by doing this routing. The problems in making this a reality were manifold:

Adam's company needed specialized 45' containers which were not very easily available and Adam's company gobbled them up at an astonishing rate.

The man-lift equipment pieces were very heavy and yet delicate, and so the blocking and bracing needed for rail required extra work to prevent "rail humping" which was when container rail cars would bump into each other due to traveling or linking/delinking from other rail cars. If the man-lift equipment was not blocked/braced well enough, the damage (and subsequent damage claims of their clients) would skyrocket!

The exercise of railing them from West Coast to East Coast and making the intermodal connections precisely and then catching the intended vessels (on the East Coast) was very nearly at an accuracy level akin to clockwork.

The project had many possible pitfalls and thus was so daunting that no container line or logistics company was willing to take it on. It was hard enough to do one move and make it work, much less hundreds of moves in a month.

Whether it was overreaching ambition or plain stupidity, when I learned that this was something that Adam really, really wanted, I set out to see if it could be done. But for me, the lure of the thick profit margins times multiples of tens and maybe even hundreds of moves per month was too irresistible.

After many, many meetings and lunches and "blue sky" discussions of how this could be done with both the client and my operations team, we (Adam, Turner, and I) decided it could be done, although it was going to be very difficult initially and throughout the process. There was a day when I thought we had, at least theoretically, crossed all the

"T's and dotted all the I's". We started with a few 45' containers for the initial bookings and then we put them on the railcars after Adam's crew dutifully blocked/braced the man-lift equipment as if they were newly born babies put gently into their cribs.

The containers moved out and made all the connections, which we watched like a hawk. Anytime anything even remotely resembled a snarl would show up, Turner was on the phone barking out demands for ETAs and ETDs. When the initial loads showed up on the East Coast, we had to make sure that most, if not all, of the 45' containers holding the man-lifts were stowed in the "hot stow" position which was a position on the ships which were highly coveted because they were the first ones to be offloaded when the ship hit its destinations.

It was a HUGE triumphant moment when I received word that the containers reached their European destinations with NO DAMAGE CLAIMS!

From then on, the moves miraculously (and I do mean that literally) moved very much like clockwork! We were rewarded with volumes that hovered around 40 to 47 moves a week! This made our team instant heroes, not only in the eyes of the client, but also my company's management! Needless to say, it was a very profitable project for my division!

Remember in Chapter 7: The Misunderstandings Over "Value" I had a Personal Case Citing: When I Mistook Pricing for "Value"? Well, there is an epilogue to that story as well which involves the incomparable Ms. Jones!

Personal Case Citing – "Tested Metal"

Ms. Jones had already done many successful logistical moves with me for about six months when one day she called me up to have a meeting. She stated that they had a new move being planned to move their goods to Asia from the same border town that we did the European moves. She was a bit nervous as this was something that they had not done before but, because my company really lived up to every bit of what we said we could do for the European moves, she gave me first right of refusal for this new move. No RFPs or bid tenders. If I could do these new moves, she would give it to me. I could and we did. We added more volume from her company to our growing list of happy clients and their precious business!

Why no bids? Because we were tested metal in battle and we performed what we said we could do. Life is good!

Okay, that's it! This is the crux of The Honorable Relationship teachings! When you look back and see how it works and the almost irresistible dynamism of the underlying precepts, then all that is left to do is to plan well and execute based on what was covered!

The strength of The Honorable Relationship is that you are using innately human emotions and characteristics that transcend any "technique" or fad and co-opting them towards your plans.

Napoleon once said, and I am paraphrasing, that the hardest part of war was the planning and the easy part was to just do it! I could not have said it better. Plan out and then do. If there are misfires, examine what went wrong and re-deploy. It is just as simple as that. **The next section has some observations that seek to puncture the myths of current day business thinking...**

Chapter 24:
Contrarian Model

How do you use "conventional" wisdom against itself? That is to say, there are things that most organizations do that block you from getting to their real decision makers. If you think/act beyond the readily visible world, then you may avoid being shunted off. Here are some quick rules:

- Using the client's bureaucracy to inculcate yourself

- The Power of No

- The Meaning of the Long Lunch

- The True Meaning of "Guanxi"

Look at the overall landscape of what your industry is doing and how it works. If you examine what others are doing, you will begin to see the patterns that we spoke of in Chapter 1,the patterns that create "pack mentality" which leads to mediocrity. Is that what you want?

If it is not what you seek, then you must use different lenses to see your world. What are some popularly held paradigms and why do they exist? When you see them, do the exact opposite.

1. Using the client's bureaucracy to inculcate yourself

As we spoke of earlier, RFPs, procurement departments and the lot are meant to keep you out, not necessarily to bring you in (see Chapter 8: What Does the Client Really Want? – Decision Branch 2). But what if you were to use them for your own good? How can you make the process more inclined to work for you rather than against you?

First, remember, someone is reading the stuff that you are sending out to determine whether you are worthy to receive their business. Write the RFP response in such a way as to make it a guided tour. Give summaries, put in pictures, Visio diagrams, and other visual aids that will help the process along by alleviating reading a mountain of dry text with even drier statistics and numbers.

Using case studies and citing real life examples is key to giving the reader the overwhelming impression that you actually have done the work and know what you are talking about, which is sometimes the tipping point.

Always engage (whenever possible) with a Client Champion who may guide you in the process of what their company does (or does not) like in an RFP response. This may not be an option but, if it is, then use it.

When in front of a selection committee, do not do "Death by PowerPoint", I beg of you!! Reading line by line a 64 slide deck of PPT is not going to win you anything. What really works is when your presentation (with or without PowerPoint) draws the selection committee into a discussion and elicits questions that may be answered by both sides. This is where you can tell if you have a ghost of a chance of winning. If the committee is combative with you, that does not necessarily mean that you are losing the bid. Some members may have that type of style of confrontational approach or may genuinely not like your company due to previous problems. If you field these questions with professionalism and concise, non-evasive but effective answers, it will help to go a long way to dispel former perceptions.

However, if you have an apathetic crowd of folks that do not have much to ask or say, then your chances are pretty low of winning. Sorry.

Another way to distinguish yourself from others is to propose alternative thinking, processes, and pricing than the ones that were proffered or asked by the RFP. This is not to say you don't answer them on what they wanted – you should do that. However, offering one or two ideas that may be variants of the theme or radical departures of the RFP could demonstrate to the selectors that you have ideas that may be adoptable and that you have invested creative energies, whereas most of your competitors probably have not done so (90% will not).

The key is to project yourself into the decision maker's mind as to what they think is important, whether it be a certain approach, a type of service or product, an alignment with certain companies that would represent the client well in its workings, etc. This is why working on a blind RFP (one in which you do not know any of the principals well) is really a waste of time and resources that has NEVER paid off in terms of efficacious use of people and resources.

If you do win an RFP, then service the heck out of it and keep that level of excellence because it is so much easier to have the client stay with you than to try to get a new vending partner. Keep in mind that the clients also hate the procurement process (maybe even more than you do).

2. The Power of No

For most of us, we have been conditioned from early on to say "yes" to people and not "no" if only because "yes" usually elicits a positive response from the other party that you have just said yes to.

"No", on the other hand, is deemed negative and is never used in client management as most people see it. Why? Because "no", or any push back, will cause displeasure and that is something to be avoided with clients, whether they be current or potential. The cardinal rule for client management is to accommodate the client whenever possible under the banner of "The Customer is King" or "The Customer is Always Right". I strongly differ from this servile type of thinking as this only promotes the kind of thinking that creates the inequity that I spoke of in earlier chapters. In an Honorable Relationship, there should be as close to parity in the power continuum as possible situation. To have the client be so much higher is egregious. This is not to say that I am not aware that a client has power in the form of purchasing power; however, he/she is also dependent on you in providing a needed service and product.

But what about the client that is a bully or dysfunctional client? You know the kind I am talking about. Just in case you have forgotten the various manifestations of this type of cretin, then let me illustrate some examples:

- The client that wants you to submit to very difficult terms of sales (payment dates, penalties disguised as service level agreement clauses, billing procedures, termination notices, surcharges and fees). The client does NOT view you as a trusted and necessary partner in their success but instead treats you terribly.

- The client that threatens to give your business to someone else should you displease them or not hit the "metrics". There is always a threat that you are not going to be working for them very long should you not perform at their pleasure. The operative underlying thinking is that there are plenty of people right behind you that will fill up the void if/when you are gone.

- The client that always second guesses you and asks/demands concessions from you in the way of pricing, extra product/services, payment terms, etc. This client's approach is invariably win/lose with you losing and him winning. It may not be in bold strokes but rather small requests (at first) that only increase and gain momentum as you continue your relationship with them. For every concession you make, the more emboldened this type of person will become in seeking more "gimmes" from you.

- The client that does not live up to their word. They offer you a contract (verbally) for 10,000 units but when it comes time to work through the written portion, the rates go down to 8,500 units or 5,000 units due to some circumstances that are beyond their control. Maybe once is excusable but recurring patterns are not good signs. If their word is like the wind, how can they be trusted to be sound, steady, and honorable business partners? The answer is that they cannot.

- The client that is overly dependent on you to the point you are devoting a great deal of your time and resources to this account with no appreciable return in increased business or benefit. This may be justified by many as doing good account managing but this is a self-made smokescreen in that these types of clients are vampires. Vampires are parasitic and live off the host/donor to the detriment of the host/donor. They don't help or add value to your world as a vending partner. They will feed off of you until you draw the line and then they move onto the next "victim".

In the recitation of these various types of dysfunctional relationships in business, you might have seen some similarities of past, current or potential clients that you know. The answer is a very small but powerful word called "No". No to severely inequitable contracts, no to undue pressure and one-sided transactions, and certainly no to dishonorable actions and treatment by the client. You have that power. You really do. You just need to exercise it judiciously.

The power of no may seem difficult especially in light of possibly staggering volumes and revenues; however, it has been my experience that the pleasure derived from acquiring these types of clients (much like sin) is a short season.

The counter argument is that their business is so valuable in a down market or any market that it would be folly to reject doing business with them. On an empirical and quantifiable scale, that may be true and if this is the reason why you have chosen to touch the "hot iron" by doing business with these entities with full knowledge that they have these terrible attributes, then most business managers would support you.

Your company's business managers would support you because it is not they themselves who are going to go through the pain and grief of dealing with these terrible people. It is you. But if it were just a matter of shying away from doing the difficult and not that there are real good business reasons to NOT engage with these people, then I would tell you so. However, I am not loathe of doing the hard, dirty work involved in getting clients. On the contrary, I usually tread where most people fear to go. I have no fear in this regard.

No, my argument in not doing business with these types of people is that they are not going to benefit your company beyond a short time (a year, a contract term, ???). Some may take this as an acceptable rationale in taking on such clients because they will get something for a period of time at the very least. But, much like doing a deal with the devil, if you get into bed with these types, you will only suffer and in the end lose your soul (autonomy).

I cannot tell you the litany of examples that have populated my life experiences in seeing others wreck themselves in the pursuit of these terrible accounts all for the benefit of their short term "wins". In the end, they were punished for their participation and became very bitter in the process.

And what about that vaunted business that foolish client managers drool over? First, isn't it funny that these bullies tend to be larger accounts that promise big revenue dollars and can back them up? It seems an unwritten rule that the bigger some of these firms become, the more demanding (sometimes in an over-the-top-way) they become?!

So you are willing to ignore all the hints of the perverse evil that will befall you and then you go full bore to get the business from Monolith Inc.'s Daru division. Let me play this out for you in four stages:

Stage 1:

After working hard to sharpen the pencil and taking cuts to get a thread bare margin, you win the mega volume and revenue contract (one year in length). The announcement is heralded within your organization and you are an overnight star!

Your company then goes about to fulfill the contract on the start date.

Stage 2:

You are performing well overall in terms of fulfilling the contract; however, due to the dysfunctionalisms listed previously, the going is getting harder and harder to fulfill. But you are determined to hold onto that hot iron.

Now, because the client knows you are very much dependent on them, he/she will keep on raising the bar for you to constantly hurdle. This comes in terms of further pricing concessions (even before contract expiration), payment terms, extra services/product features, more of your company resources to be devoted to the further maintenance of the client, etc.

Usually at this juncture, you will be starting to wonder if this account is worth all the pressure, constant barraging, and threatening tones. However, there is a problem. Your increased volume and revenues, which may have an inverse profit margin due to the various demands and concessions that you gave into, is now a fairly large piece of your total business. (Remember that you became your company's hero in landing Monolith's account.)

Stage 3:

You get a sinking feeling that even IF you wanted to walk away from this abusive client, you cannot. Why? He/she is simply too big in your universe now. So you are now seeing the trap that was set and that you are doing your best to get out of. You cannot replace Monolith's business so easily because they are such a large footprint to fill.

Right about now, there should be a sense of dread and panic setting in. It's like owing money to the mob. You feel trapped because, with each passing day, you get more and more pressure applied to you by the abusive client and it has now become your number one issue to the detriment of your other clients, new prospects and even some core functions that you need to carry out.

Stage 4:

I need to tell you of the inevitable last stage and it involves the "hard" moment. The "hard" moment is the point in time that you can no longer make any more concessions to the client to satisfy him. Someone else or a group of someone else's start to take your place in volume levels and revenue because they are able to better do so or are not as beaten up and emotionally drained as you and your company are. Usually the coup de grace is administered fairly bloodlessly as you are jettisoned with a lot of anger, bitterness, fatigue and a huge hole in your production that you now have to fill. Your "stock" goes to zero very quickly as soon as this happens.

Still think that this scenario is worth it? Think again.

Personal Case Citing – When David said "NO" to Goliath

As I related the story from a Personal Case Citing: One in a million shot from Chapter 11: Homework, my company had one the very large contract from a giant electronic printer and peripherals company. Now a year later, this client wanted to re-negotiate the contract due to a spurious reason that they cited.

I then went through a three-month hellish process of contract work wherein all the hoops that the procurement department thought of was unleashed on me and my company. While this was happening, I reached out to the real business owner (i.e., the budget owner), Talmadge, who had insulated himself from this process by using the procurement department as a buffer.

Talmadge said that it was best to follow protocol of his company's re-negotiation process and work exclusively with them and not him. I did not like that answer but left it at that.

When we were asked to give our pricing proposal, I gave a pricing schema that was higher than that which was on the previously nullified contract. Then I turned it in. I knew that the client would not like this at all.

After a silent week, I got a call from the procurement person who said that they had a problem with my pricing of the 16 European, Middle Eastern and African (EMEA) markets that they got from me. I acted coy and asked them what the issue was. The procurement person said that my pricing was to go down, not up, from the previous contract. I said that this was not in the cards. Our rates, due to inflation and currency fluctuations, could not go down or else it was not good for us. The procurement person seemed perplexed with me and my attitude because I don't think he heard the "no" word very often in his role with the company.

I then hung up the phone and called Talmadge. I couldn't reach him right away as he was very busy. One week became three weeks and the deadline of the contract signing was only a week away. The procurement people and some of Talmadge's staff were hounding me to submit to their request and then get it signed. I gave them all very vague responses in the order of "we are still working on it".

I finally reached Talmadge and put it to him straight:

John (J): "I don't want to work through the Jimmy the procurement guy anymore."

Talmadge (T): "John, you don't understand. That is how we do things around here."

(J): Not how I do things. Look, you have the ultimate say in this matter and I want you to work with me on this or else it won't get done in time by going through intermediaries. You are old school and so am I. Let's get it done the right way – between the two of us."

(T): "John, okay but your request for increase in all 16 world markets is not going to fly."

(J): "Why not?"

Talmadge snorted a laugh.

(T): "Because you can't go up, you need to go down or else we need to seek other options."

(J): "Okay, let's talk. Do you like our work?"

(T): "Yes, very much so. You guys are effective."

(J): "Good and thanks! So, if you like our work and you think we are effective, and we really are effective because we have shattered all the metrics you have given us over the past year, then why are you willing to jeopardize this level of work by nickel and diming us?"

(T): "What do you mean by that?"

(J): "What I mean is that your company is putting costs before efficacy and I think you know what the result will be. Disastrous. Do not kid yourself. For every bit you cut or seek to get from us, the quality of the work will suffer commensurately if not geometrically."

(T): "I see your point but you can't win in all 16 markets I know my people. You'll need to take it on the chin on some of them."

(J): "Okay, what markets do you want us to take a hit on?"

(T): "Two markets (which he named)."

(J): "Let me think about it, okay?"

(T): "Okay."

I then re-priced the two markets a shade lower but kept the other 14 markets at the higher rates. The client decision maker, Talmadge, approved it and we won the contract at higher rates which shocked a lot of my own company's internal folks because of the size and market strength of this client.

---

3. The Meaning of Long Lunches.

In the 40s, 50s and 60s, account executives in America used to take out their clients to long three martini lunches. As in shows like "Mad Men", these were usually drink fests that had little to do with business but more into ingratiating yourself to the client which may be a form of business development come to think of it.

While I think such behavior may have been more "fun" than productive, there is something to long lunches (sans alcohol) that produces much fruit. I am loathe to take clients out to dinner because I really enjoy my evenings and away-from-work time. I don't think that clients usually would consent to dinners as well due to the aforementioned reasons or others.

However, lunches, especially longer lunches (1-2 hours), are an important tool to understand your client in a context that is professional (lunches during the work day) and yet creates the right level of intimacy.

How to use them to really learn about your client is the key. Here are some ideas that are borne from experience:

- Whenever possible, take the current or potential client out to lunch at a top notch restaurant. It does not need to be a 3-star Michelin restaurant but a better-than-Applebee's type will do. Why? Because that type of restaurant (whether someone says so or not) impresses. It also shows that you have good taste and are at a certain social level.

NOTE: even in this age of propriety, if the client pays for his share, then you still come out ahead in terms of image projection.

- Do not drink. If the client drinks, then so be it. At most, one beer or wine if the client insists as this doesn't put him/her in an awkward position. But no more than that. Keeping your head clear is key and you don't want to create an image of being a drinking buddy type.

- Talk very little about business, if at all. In fact, spend more time talking about him/her and their world. What interests them? Their latest or last vacation destination? Their family? Their educational background and what they thought of it? Their proudest moments in life? Gather as much information as to what drives this person. The drivers that propel and motivate a person are key to finding out what works and doesn't work when working with them on projects, etc. as was mentioned in Chapter 8: Know Thy Client's iceberg analogy of hidden drivers.

- Find out more about his/her personality and perceptions. Is he/she more careful and security driven? Or is he/she more driven by risk and reward? How does he/she perceive the world and events in it? Are they cynical and jaded types or are they more optimistic and hopeful?

Where in the continuum of thinking are they located in areas such as:

Conservative versus Liberal

Hyper versus Sedate

Narcissistic versus Self Deprecating

Humble versus Proud

NOTE: You easily do this for others in your life such as friends and family matters and I am betting that you haven't gotten to this point in your life without a fair bit of ability to gauge and react to others in a way that allows you to manage various types of personality.

- Besides knowing facts and figures of their lives (spouse's name, children's' ages and names, etc.), you want to find out the essence of the person as much as you can. What makes this person tick? What are prime motivators or events in this person's life that rationalizes this person's world?

- Why lunch? Why can't you do this anywhere else such as the person's office? Because there is a dynamic about breaking bread with someone that affords you an intimacy that far extends beyond the facts and figures of people and transactions. The mere fact that you are not at the person's office takes them away from the defense lines that people erect to block out this type of intimacy and access.

Personal Case Citing – The Power of the Conversation

I once went to interview for a sales marketing position a major security consultancy with the president. The position was not a posted one but I asked if there was an opportunity to interview for such a role. I was granted that by the president.

The meeting was held at the worldwide headquarters in New Jersey and I lived in the Washington, D.C. area at that time. I crammed my mind with all sorts of data on the company and all relevant industry information prior to the meeting.

When I met with president, I found him to be very affable and friendly but deadly smart. We talked initially about my family and life background. I thought this was fairly routine "ice breaking" conversation prior to the meat of the interview. But when the conversation kept going on about world views, history of China, the relative young ages of the new powershakers of the world, etc. well into an hour, I realized that the president had no intention of talking about my job, my fit into the company or any of that.

After two and a half hours, we adjourned leaving me to wonder what this whole exercise was all about. Had I wasted my time and costs to get up to New Jersey?

I then was asked to interview with other people, in a series of interviews that lasted for nine months. Yes, you read correctly – 9 months! I interviewed with seven others in various departments and roles.

I was absolutely frustrated as to what they were doing but I was very intrigued at the same time. Finally I told the president that it was time to tell me what this was all about.

The president said that he was trying to fit me into the company but that they simply didn't have a sales marketing director level role. So he was trying to see what area he could get me into the firm. His last remark was, "I am really going to be upset if you leave your present company and work for someone else and that we've blown an opportunity for you to come and work here!" I was stunned. He had that much interest and faith in me. I was also very flattered, if not confused.

Then, two weeks later, I got a phone call from Tom, the Vice President of Sales and Marketing, and he asked me if I would like to have lunch. We were to meet at a very swank restaurant which was half way between us in Wilmington, Delaware. I said yes and laughingly told him that this would be my eighth interview thus far. He apologized for that but I certainly wanted to see this to the end!

I met Tom, who was very friendly and straight forward, and once again we talked about my family and the difference in living on the East Coast versus the West Coast and his family and so on and so on. This was becoming very surreal but I went along with it nonetheless.

At the end of the two and a half hour lunch, again we never even touched on the job, my qualifications and any possible fit opportunities. I then had to ask.

John (J): "Tom, I must ask you what you folks think of my ability to do the job if there was a sales management position and if so what would it be."

Tom (T): "I think that you would be a good fit and..."

(J) (interrupting him): "But we never even talked about this. You and the president have never even asked any questions regarding the job!"

(T): "We know from your resume that you can probably do the job really well, but our firm is very particular on whom it brings on, and so we really want to get to know the 'real' John Lee."

(J): "What do you think my chances are?"

(T): "Good (he said as he smiled)."

I wanted to ask him what I was interviewing for because I lost track of what they were thinking of doing. But I did not ask. Confused, I went home and told my wife and prayed for guidance from God as to what the next steps were to be.

One week later, I got a call from Tom who then offered me a newly created position of Vice President of Sales (working under Tom) at a starting salary and benefits package that was two pay grades above my current position! I was elated to say the least and I accepted shortly thereafter.

In looking back, I realized what was happening. They were interviewing me to find out more about the real John Lee instead of all the nonsense that people throw out in interviews. They wanted to know if I was able to do the job and be able to really work and play well with them in a brand new position that they had created using the knowledge they had of me.

It worked out marvelously! It has been the best job of my life and I have been extremely effective and happy in this company!! None of that would have happened had they not gotten a good "read" from me by asking about the person behind the façade! God is great!

---

4. The True Meaning of "Guanxi" (Chinese for relationship)

As more and more Western companies are trying to inculcate themselves into Asia (more specifically, China), the word "guanxi" keeps popping up in the business world and its literature. Like most of China, the word is very old and very complex in its meaning. Most Western literature has defined guanxi as something akin to a warm and fuzzy relationship based on trust and knowledge.

And while these are definite components of guanxi, the real meaning is far deeper and more serious than what most Western literature and thinking has attributed to it.

For starters, guanxi as it is practiced is radically different from the textbook definitions and examples given by most writers. Guanxi is about balance of terrors between two parties and a healthy respect of the capabilities of each other. Much like a Joan Rivers comedy routine that I once saw in which Joan explained that she's always had a "painless dentist". And how she ensured that she did was, when he bent over to work on her mouth, Joan would reach over and grab his testicles in one hand and say "Now we aren't going to hurt each other, are we?"

If that sounds a bit harsh for most readers who have not done business in Asia, know that this is a fair assessment of how things are done. It's not racist. It's not xenophobic. It's real. I happen to be ¾ Chinese and ¼ Ukrainian by birth and grew up in a very strict traditional Chinese family in the US so this vantage point has given me insights into how business and relations are done and kept in US and in China (Asia). I say China (Asia) because the Chinese have their own version of the Diaspora just as much as the Jews and Irish. Driven by economic and political reasons, the Chinese people have come to populate all of Asia and, in doing so, have brought their own cultural form of doing business. This in turn has influenced the way a lot of Asia does business because of the Chinese influence.

While it is true that it is regarded as crass to have just met someone and then try to get down to "brass tacks" to do business in most of the non-Western world especially Asia, it is also true that Asian business people are just as pragmatic and "down to brass tacks" as any hardboiled US business man or woman. How they conduct that business diverges greatly from Western society. The point of knowing someone before diving into business is to see if their future "partner" is able to withstand the stresses and strains of business far beyond what is represented in proof of concept papers, PowerPoint presentations, and statements of work (SOWs).

They also want to test your vulnerabilities to see if there are any to take advantage of. Are there any Achilles heels that can be uncovered either in the individuals or the organizations in which an upper hand may be gotten in doing business.

You see, it is all about win/lose. The concept of win/win is fairly nonexistent in Asian business dealings. This doesn't mean that they want to do business so that you suffer loss or are greatly hurt – who would consent to that? However, Asian thinking is that I must "win" or at least win more than you. That is to say, they seek to have an advantage somewhere that makes them know that they have the "best deal" that they can strike.

That is why bribes, kickbacks and corruption are so rampant in Asia. It is to have the upper hand, the inside track. Though all the laws state that this is illegal and not to be tolerated, there is a blind eye that is turned to these events as long as it is not overt and doesn't harm the overall public safety. Why do you think there are so many product tamperings and safety issues emanating from Asia as opposed to many Western countries? The cost cuttings and short cuts to do business to get ahead and stay ahead are the vehicles being driven by this overarching need to win. This is not to say that Western business leaders are without sin because that would be untruthful.

Winning is only one aspect of the ethos. The other one is to test the partners. You cannot truly let your guard down in doing business in Asia for, if you do, you will find yourself in a very difficult position.

Personal Case Citing – The Newbie at Guanxi

When I was just starting out in international business waters as a logistics account executive, I was courting a Los Angeles-based major Chinese shipper. He was a huge wastepaper shipper into Asia. Wastepaper is one of the commodities that US ships to Asia in huge bulk amounts.

I was talking extensively with Mr. Hu, who was the elder statesman of the Asian wastepaper shipping industry in Los Angeles (and had a lot of power) about getting a piece of his business, which was huge (5,000 containers a month worth of volume). My company had never had a share of this business so I was breaking into uncharted waters (pardon the pun). Mr. Hu took a liking to me and consented to give me 1,000-container run over a contract period of six months, which was a huge leap of volume for my company that never had a stick of business from him. I was in seventh heaven as Mr. Hu signed the contract. My company managers were elated and thought I was a hero for breaking so solidly into this account. I basked in the glow!

One week later, to the day, I received a phone call from Mr. Hu and this is what took place.

Mr. Hu: "John! John! I have some bad news to tell you."

John: "What is it Mr. Hu?" (as my stomach was knotting up)

Mr. Hu: "John, I just was paid a visit by your competitor, Behemoth Shipping, and they said they can lower the price of carrying my freight by $50 a metric ton less than the contract we signed last week."

John: "Oh, but…"

Mr. Hu: "John, you need to match this price."

John: "Mr. Hu, I cannot go back to my pricing folks so soon into this contract to ask for such a quantum decrease in the contract."

Mr. Hu: "John, you must or else I cannot deliver on this contract."

John: "Mr. Hu, a contract is a contract and you need to honor it."

Mr. Hu: "John, I can only honor a contract that I can deliver on. I cannot conduct business at $50/metric ton more. That is no way for me to do business!"

John: "Mr. Hu, that price we negotiated last week was very cutting edge and very low and you admitted to this yourself. Now all of a sudden you get a visit from my competition and suddenly you cannot deliver? I find that hard to believe."

Mr. Hu: "John, I do not want to argue with you! You know what you must do!"

John: "Mr. Hu, I cannot lower the price and if you won't deliver, then I guess we'll have to settle it legally."

Mr. Hu: "John, John, John, you will not win if you go the lawyer route. For every one lawyer you produce, I have twenty. Also, do you want your name to be cast in a bad light in this industry in which I have a lot of say?"

John: (controlling my fury) "Mr. Hu, I will see what I can do."

Mr. Hu: "Good boy – you try!"

I hung up the phone puzzled, angry and dejected. I did not mention this conversation to the higher-ups in my company because they were relying on me to deliver the 1,000 containers as is. For the better part of the day, I felt a foreboding sense of doom in terms of my future and career with the company. I felt I was being setup by Mr. Hu, which was the case. How could Mr. Hu magically have a competitor of mine come up and offer a phenomenal rate reduction ($50/metric ton) if he had not told or shown them my contract inked last week? He had to have relayed this to them in order to extort a lower rate for himself. I was furious.

I then called my father (living in Seattle at the time), whom I refer to as the Chinese of Chinese. If anyone would know how to deal with Chinese businessmen, it would be my father who was a very smart, sharp businessman before he became a Christian minister. I told him about the situation and he listened very carefully and attentively. After my recitation of the situation, I asked my Dad what he thought I should do. My Dad said simply, "Son, do to him what he did to you."

I thought about it a minute and then asked what he meant by that. My dad said, "Son, I don't know your business but reverse what he did to you and do it back to him!"

What my father said made perfect sense but I did not know how I could turn the tables on such a powerful man. I thought about it all evening and into the night. Despairing of any solution, I went to sleep miserable. I prayed to God for guidance prior to sleep and then passed out from sheer exhaustion!

As I was sleeping, it came to me in my dreams. I woke up the next morning (which was unusually bright and sunny) and thanked God for the answer!

I got to the office, got a cup of coffee and called Mr. Hu.

John: "Mr. Hu."

Mr. Hu: "Yes, John! Can you do it? Can you match Behemoth's quote?"

John: "Yes Mr. Hu I can match Behemoth's quote."

Mr. Hu: "Good boy!! I knew you could do it. You are American but first and foremost you are Chinese!"

John: "But wait, Mr. Hu. You need to know that if I do the match, you need to give me double the volume stated on the contract which is 2,000 containers in six months."

Mr. Hu: "Oh no! I cannot do this, John! You are killing me! I have many commitments and contracts and if I do this, it will hurt my other commitments."

John: "Mr. Hu, this latest twist is hurting me and my company so we need for you to share the pain. And besides, you go to the bathroom to take a crap and 5,000 containers come out!"

Silence. Long silence.

Mr. Hu: (Laughing heartily) "Okay, okay! Good boy! (Still laughing) You have a deal!"

I smiled as well. I just doubled the phenomenal volume for my company albeit at a lower price but they would consent to do this for such a powerful shipper and for our first real victory in gaining his business! Through God's guidance, along with my father's insight, I was able to turn the tables on Mr. Hu and still keep a congenial relationship!

It was then that I began to understand the win/lose playbook that Mr. Hu was using and the need to test the relationship. Mr. Hu could easily have fulfilled the contract with me regardless of the circumstances but he wanted to test me and my mettle.

Since then I have had a myriad of business dealings in Asia, Europe, South America, etc., and have learned from each one. However, the next critical learning came from a lecture given by a Chinese businessman and trade delegate to a group of US politicians and businessman. I attended the session with no particular expectations. However, what I got from that brief afternoon lecture in Washington, D.C. opened up my eyes forever.

The speaker stepped up to the podium to present his views of East/West businesses and the ways of doing business. He was throwing out anecdotes and statistics until he said the following statement "In the West, the contract is the relationship. In the East, the relationship is the contract." WOW! To say it was a seismic shock is to understate the impact of that statement because it struck me like a body blow! When he said that, I looked over at a colleague and we both grinned from ear to ear. It was like scales falling off of my eyes as this man, in such a succinct and wonderfully crafted statement, distilled all the mish mash of experiences into a concise dictum. This truly was how the relationships are treated in Asia and other old world regions!

That statement explained why it was that Mr. Hu treated the contract that we had inked a week ago as nothing but a piece of paper. There was no magical status of importance conferred upon the contract as it would have been in the West. The contract was just the opening gambit (the first step) of a relationship and not the ultimate manifestation of the relationship.

That is also why, subsequent to that speaker's presentation, I could see the frustration of Western businessmen and women when confronted with Asian business people who signed the "sacrosanct" contract and then began to change terms and conditions of the contract even before the ink was dried! It is this fundamental difference that, once perceived, allows you to see the radical differences between Asian thinking of contracts and negotiations from their US and European counterparts! I have also found this to be true in other old world cultures that do not look at the contract as the final arbiter of conduct in business dealings.

Paraphrasing Sun Tzu in the "Art of War" which was written many millennia ago, you have to know the terrain or landscape in which you are about to conduct war (business) in order to be able to win the battle and the war. By the way, reading the "Art of War" is a great primer to begin to understand how Eastern thinking operates.

In the traditional Western business world teachings, there seems to be a rightness and wrongness to things that drives the ethos and operative paradigms. But in Asia, it is not necessarily that as much as answering the question of: is it feasible or not? This is not to say that Asians have no morals (that is not what I am saying). There is a very utilitarian pragmatism that informs all business decisions which is hard to fathom coming from the West. Let me give a very pervasive example. The subject is corruption, especially the official kind of corruption.

Corruption exists in all cultures and societies. To think otherwise is to be stupid and naïve. However, in Asia, the various cultures have dealt with it in an equally fatalistic and functional basis. In order to operate successfully and to do well in the various levels of these cultures, one must know how to navigate adeptly. From varying levels of governmental office holders to many levels of business partners and suppliers, they all have their agendas.

To try to go through these societies without confronting some form of graft, kickback or old fashioned palm greasing is to be unrealistic! Why? Because the hand that is stuck out for payment has been hardwired into these societies for millennia, and just because your compliance officer says that you must never do certain things, doesn't mean it doesn't exist all around you.

These societies are conditioned throughout the millennia to factor this into their lives and their conduct. There is an allowance for this in their dealings and their lives. People have incorporated and factored this into their business dealings. No one really likes it but they know that this is what is needed in order to get things done.

That is why Western businesses (that have their own issues back home) are constantly trying to reconcile the good, righteous and well-meaning Western laws of anti-corruption that they are mandated to follow versus the Asian environment of co-opting corruption that they find themselves in. To kick against it with a zero tolerance policy has created and will continue to create roadblocks, problems and failures for businesses. This is a hard thing to say, however, if we are to be honest then we must admit that there is this practice.

This is just one illustration that there are some fundamental and quantum differences in the ways various peoples perform business and life functions. To not consider this in your own response to such societies is to be foolish and unprepared.

The Contrarian Model is not advocating to do things in a contrarian or opposite way from what is currently being taught just to be different or trendy. That is absolutely to be avoided! However, the Contrarian Model seeks to have you question deeply what we take as operative thinking. Why do we do the things that we do? Why do we do things the way we do them?

Remember from Chapter 1 that people, animals, and the physical world all follow patterns. But are these pre-set patterns always the most effective way of doing things? Or are they done because they are "safe" and "comfortable"? If history has taught nothing, at least it teaches us that humans innovate and iterate and, with each evolutionary twist, we are propelled further up the chain of efficiency and efficacy.

Question what EVERYONE takes for granted. Take things apart and examine how things can be reconfigured to be so much better. That is the kind of innovative thinking that blasts through mediocre efforts and results!

Chapter 25:
Endgame

Now that you have been introduced to The Honorable Relationship, the next appropriate question to ask is: now what? What will you do with this new (but old) business approach? I would like to leave you with parting thoughts on how The Honorable Relationship may be better utilized in getting you what you are trying to achieve.

- First and foremost, you must understand that people work in patterns. It is as fundamental as gravity. These patterns can block and hinder you or they can be understood so as to co-opt them for your own good. This book seeks to have you see something that everyone takes for granted, to see with new lenses the stuff that is there in plain sight every day -- that organizations and people work in very tired old patterns of engagement. However, when new dynamics or changes occur to change old paradigms, the peculiar thing is that people generally do change these patterns in reaction to them until it is absolutely necessary or plainly evident (remember the 12 Strong Forces?) If this statement were not true, then I would say that most booth exhibitors at conventions would not re-up year after year to stand there waiting for "customers". And yet they do.

- You need to know the underlying reason why people (clients) do what they do. What drives them? If you follow the cascading approach of Knowledge – Understanding Use Value – Relationship – Exploration, you will be able to discern this. However, if you approach client work as a mechanical, technique driven and transaction based effort, you will not get beyond the true factors for success in obtaining and keeping clients. You will then run with the rest of the pack, but is that what you really want? Or rather would you like to go your own way and be a leader in your field?

- You are your own brand. You cannot depend upon others to help or bolster your image/brand. That is something uniquely your own and you must work hard at perfecting it and making it better, more effective and more recognized and respected. Relegating your personal branding to others (be they your own company's efforts or industry's initiatives) is like having someone else raise and rear your own children. Would you do that? I don't think so. And like a child, your personal brand takes time to mature and gather strength, especially at the outset. But you will be amazed at the rapidity of progress if you devote time, attention, and effort to build up and nurture your branding with your current and potential clients.

- Lastly, there are no short cuts in the process. You need to build the platform as outlined in this book so as to create a stable baseline whence to begin your own World Domination Program. In fact, The Honorable Relationship is a form of a short cut in that it involves leveraging of existing relationships to take you higher, faster, and farther than you could achieve with gimmicky programs or systems.

The main thrust of The Honorable Relationship is to help you pole vault past the competition and sustain the lead that you have created by making your and your company nearly indispensable to your clients. When you can achieve that level of performance, then you really can gain and retain clients "forever" or at least indefinitely.

One thing I insist for you to do: follow the program as outlined and give it the best shot you have for six months and see if it doesn't do what I claim it can do. Much like an old family recipe, it is best to follow the procedures verbatim at first. During that time, you will find certain things work better than others for you or your particular situation, but stick with the program as is.

After six months, you can re-evaluate to see efficacy and effort. Why six months? Because then you can really get the full effect of your efforts without dilution and distraction. Then, like an old family recipe, you can "season to taste" or adjust the program to your liking.

Please remember one thing. As with the cover design showing that a little pebble can outweigh (outdo) the big rock, then you can outweigh or outdo the biggest opponents. You just have to believe in yourself and put the ideas into action. The forthcoming Honorable Relationship workbook will help you as well.

Okay, that's it! You are well on your way to creating a very powerful career with very dramatic results!

Good hunting and God speed!

Exhibit 1 – Line of Questioning

Company/Division/Dept?

Contact person's name/title/location/contact information (office, mobile, fax, email)?

The overall growth of the company? What markets does it occupy? Where are areas of growth?

What are you in charge of? What is the geographical footprint?

Who do you report to? What silo is your department under? Stand alone?

Who makes the decisions on major matters? More than one decision maker?

How are decisions made

What other departments are involved in decisions?

What are some of the issues that they are currently facing?

When you do go outside of the company, what functions usually drive this?

What do you look at or for with vendor partners doing these functions?

What are areas that have not been covered that you would like to see? Why?

What are projects that you have worked on previously for your company?

What are current projects that you are working on for the company?

When does your company seek vendors? How has that worked out?

What are some of the unfinished or unresolved issues that need to be addressed within the company?

Are there any consistent "trouble areas" within the company that prevents you from having a full night of sleep?

Is there any thought of improving or changing the status quo?

Is there a budget to make the changes? Is there a political will to make changes?

Who or what is driving those changes?

Is there a budgeted amount for these changes? If so, then how are projects started?
Who are the decision makers for these projects?

Bibliography Notes

Chapter 1: Business NOT As Usual
Reality Hits Hard

1. Pfizer citing: Weintraub, Arlene. "The Doctor Won't See You Now."
   Business Week. 5 February 2007
   <http://www.businessweek.com/stories/2007-02-04/the-doctor-wont-see-
   you-now>.

2. CompUSA citing: "CompUSA to Layoff 1,800 in Sales Force". *The
   Daily Transcript.* 30 Aug. 1999 <http://www.sddt.com/News/article.
   cfm?SourceCode=19990830fak>

Chapter 2: The New Strong Forces in the Business World
Commoditization

3. "Beyond Commoditization: The Way Forward for Traditional Telecom
   Operators". *Al Bawaba News* 28 Aug. 2007
   <http://www.albawaba.com/news/beyond-commoditization-way-forward-
   traditional-telecom-operators>

4. West, Kelley. "An RFP Recipe For Success". *Document Processing
   Technology* Feb. 2007

5. "Beyond the Balanced Scorecard". *Credit Union Magazine* Aug. 2007. Vol.
   73 Issue 8, p.15

Systemization

6. Lancelot, Chris. "Chris Lancelot on...Dehumanisation of the NHS".
   GPOnline 4 April 2007 <http://web3.local.www.gponline.com/Opinion/
   article/648606/Chris-Lancelot-dehumanisation-nhs/>

7. "A Personal Touch Matters". *The Hindu Business Line* 16 July 2007
   <http://www.thehindubusinessline.com/todays-paper/tp-new-manager/
   article1687508.ece>

8. Sanders, Robert L. "Learning to say goodbye: When the records manager

turns 51". *Records Management Quarterly* 1 Oct. 1996
<http://www.accessmylibrary.com/article-1G1-18934470/learning-say-goodbye-records.html>

One-Stop-Shopping

9. Romano, Benjamin J. "Microsoft's Message to Digital Advertisers: We're building one-stop shopping". *The Seattle Times* 20 Aug. 2007
<http://community.seattletimes.nwsource.com/archive/?date=20070820&slug=videogameads20>

10. Harley, Bruce. "Electronic One-Stop Shopping: The Good, the Bad, and the Ugly". *Information Technology & Libraries* Dec. 1999 Vol. 18 Issue 4, p. 200.

Offshoring to the Global Marketplace

11. Mandel, Michael. "Which Way to the Future?" *BusinessWeek* 20 Aug. 2007
<http://www.businessweek.com/stories/2007-08-19/which-way-to-the-future>

Disposability

12. Mello, Adrian. "Choose Your Partner". *Electronic Business* 1 March 2005
<http://www.edn.com/electronics-news/4323735/Choose-your-partner>

13. Champy, Jim. "Why Partnerships Fail". *Computerworld* 20 Aug. 2001
<http://www.computerworld.com.au/article/41967/why_partnerships_fail/>

Chapter 5: Know Thyself: Seeing Things In a Different Way
CASE CITING – How Barnes & Noble won

14. Dugan, Jeanne I. "The Baron of Books". *Businessweek* 29 June 1998
<https://www.businessweek.com/1998/26/b3584001.htm>

15. Nawotka, Edward. "B&N's Leonard Riggio: Arts Patron, Collector and Artist". *Publisher's Weekly* 17 July 2003

16. Company Description. <http://www.barnesandnobleinc.com/our_company/our_company.html>

Chapter 7: The Misunderstandings Over "Value"
Case Citing – Whiz Bang!

17. Lane, Clare. "John F. Mitchell, 1928-2009: Was president of Motorola from 1980 to '95". *Chicago Tribune* June 17, 2009

18. J. Carlton Gallawa. "Who Invented Microwaves?" Copyright 1996-2007

Chapter 13: Aim and Shoot High

19. Parinello, Anthony. *Selling to VITO: The Very Important Top Officer* . Holbrook, MA: Adams Media Corporation, 1994

Chapter 21: Creating Your Own Personal Brand
Case Citing – Wine and Water

20. "Reinvigorated Bottled Water Bounces Back From Recessionary Years". *Beverage Marketing.Com* May 2012 <http://beveragemarketing. com/?section=pressreleases>

Case Citing – The Lexus Recall Story

21. Gwinne, SC, Kanise, Seiichi, Zagorin, Adam. "New Kid on the Dock". *Time Magazine* 17 Sept. 1990 <http://www.time.com/time/magazine/ article/0,9171,971153-1,00.html>

About the Author

John Lee has worked in five separate industries across all major markets (78 cities-latest count) through 30 years of market development and client management work.

Mr. Lee has worked with Fortune 500 firms in diverse world regions and has seen many variations of business and sales situations. These life and business lessons have been the proving ground to shape the thinking and methodology behind The Honorable Relationship.

Through it all Mr. Lee has learned what is real and what is not and, most importantly, what really works on the battlefield of client work and what absolutely does not work!

Mr. Lee is the CEO of LeeCore, a management consultancy, focusing on two main areas: sales force effectiveness and training and world markets business process improvement. Mr. Lee has a business degree from the University of Washington and an MBA from Seattle University.

Contact:
LeeCore
www.leecoreconsulting.com
john@leecoreconsulting.com

www.ingramcontent.com/pod-product-compliance
Lightning Source LLC
Chambersburg PA
CBHW051343200326
41521CB00014B/2467